W9-CDU-258

AMERICA AGAINST ITSELF

Other books by Richard John Neuhaus

Movement and Revolution (with Peter Berger)
In Defense of People
Christian Faith and Public Policy
Time Toward Home
To Empower People (with Peter Berger)
Freedom for Ministry
The Naked Public Square
Dispensations
Believing Today (with Leon Klenicki)
The Catholic Moment

(Books edited)

Theology and the Kingdom of God
Against the World for the World
Virtue, Public and Private
Unsecular America
Community, Confession, and Conflict
Jews in Unsecular America
Democracy and the Renewal of Education
Bible, Politics, and Democracy
Piety and Politics (with Michael Cromartie)
Guaranteeing the Good Life
Augustine Today
Niebuhr Today
American Apostasy
The Believable Futures of American Protestantism
Law and the Ordering of Our Life Together
Moral Formation and Theological Education

AMERICA AGAINST ITSELF

MORAL VISION AND THE PUBLIC ORDER

RICHARD JOHN NEUHAUS

University of Notre Dame Press

Notre Dame   London

Library of Congress Catalog-in-Publication Data

Neuhaus, Richard John.
America against itself : moral vision and the public order /
Richard John Neuhaus.
p.   cm.
Includes bibliographical references and index.
ISBN 0-268-00633-4
1. United States—Moral conditions. 2. United States—
Social conditions—1945-   I. Title.
HN90.M6N48   1992
306'.0973—dc20   91-51112
                                                        CIP

FOR CASEY KIZZIAH
Romans 8:38-39

Contents

For us, there is only the trying. The rest is not our business.

— Eliot, "East Coker"

Preface

The term *Kulturkampf* refers to a period in the 1870s when Bismarck, Chancellor of the German Empire, tried by coercive measures to reduce, if not extirpate, the influence of Catholicism. He correctly believed that Catholicism placed a check upon his aspirations to create a strong and cohesive state. America is today engaged in a relentless *Kulturkampf*, and that is what this book is about.

We could refer to what is happening as "cultural warfare." Unfortunately, in current usage "cultural warfare" suggests quarrels within the "high culture" among editors, book reviewers, dance directors, museum curators, and people who write books such as this. The high culture figures importantly in the concerns of this book. But in analyzing "America against itself," I am addressing something more fundamental and comprehensive. The word *Kulturkampf* catches it. It is a war between different ideas about who we are and who we ought to be. In conflict are different story-lines for the telling of the American democratic experiment and our place in it. Depending on who is telling the story, it sometimes seems that there are different Americas at war with one another.

As in the nineteenth-century *Kulturkampf*, religion plays a prominent part in our conflict. The contest is by no means simply one of secularists vs. religionists, although both secularists and religionists frequently portray it that way. In cultural warfare, the ideas that are most important, most binding, for all sides are religious in nature, whether

or not they are labeled "religious" ideas. Religion, we recall, is from the Latin *religo,* which means to fasten or
tie together. Religion bespeaks that which has the moral
force of obligation. The *Kulturkampf* is not, for the most
part, one of moralists vs. amoralists or immoralists. Such
a contest would be relatively clear-cut compared with our
situation. Our situation is one of moralities in conflict. It
is not surprising, therefore, that it sometimes takes on
the character of the "wars of religion" that we associate
with the sixteenth and seventeenth centuries. Surprising
to many is the fact that the conflict now brings Jews and
Christians into alliance on many fronts. That is one of the
most important developments coming out of the dialogue
between Jews and Christians of the last quarter century.

What we usually identify as religion—the religion that
dares to speak its name—is also critically important to
our present circumstance. The *Kulturkampf* is sometimes
described as between the bourgeoisie and the new knowledge class, or between the silent majority and the vol-
uble elites, or between the moral majority and secular
humanists. There is an element of truth in each of these
descriptions, no doubt. And there is more than an element
of truth in saying that it is a war between those who are
convinced that religion and religiously grounded morality
should be publicly normative and those who claim that we
are long past the time when any truth, never mind moral
truth, can be meaningfully deliberated in public.

The *Kulturkampf* in which our society is embroiled,
and will be embroiled for the foreseeable future, might
be understood as a circumstance common to all advanced
societies. Certainly, there are commonalities between our
circumstance and that of, for instance, the countries of
Western Europe. And yet, without subscribing to some of
the more extreme theories of "American exceptionalism,"
it seems obvious that America is different. The religion
factor touches on some of the more notable ways in which
America is different. G. K. Chesterton observed that America is "a nation with the soul of a church." Only in America,

many historians have noted, do we find a social order premised upon propositions. "We hold these truths," the founders declared, and then proceeded to erect a *novus ordo seclorum*, a new order for the ages.

Gallup and cooperating research agencies in Europe have done cross-cultural surveys of, among other things, "religiousness" in various countries. Among the nations of the world—measured by belief and behavior—India is the most pervasively religious society. Very close to India is the United States. At the very bottom of the list is the most thoroughly secularized society, Sweden. Peter Berger, the distinguished sociologist, has drawn from these findings a memorable apothegm: "America is a nation of Indians ruled by an elite of Swedes." That does not capture the entirety of the *Kulturkampf* by any means, but it brings us close to the heart of the matter.

In trying to understand our American battles and discontents with ourselves, I employ in the pages that follow social criticism, moral philosophy, religious reflection, and a large measure of autobiography. I would like to think that the analysis is fair, but it is certainly not dispassionate. Reason, Augustine tried to teach us 1,600 years ago, is to be passionately ordered to the truth. A rival version of reason—the disinterested, autonomous, value-neutral reason of the secular Enlightenment—is another major factor at the source of the cultural conflict under discussion. I hope that the reader will in the pages that follow come to discover why I—this particular and no doubt peculiar person—frame the questions as I do. The framing of the questions may be in some ways distinctive, but I hope not idiosyncratic. The underlying assumption in all that follows is that they are not my questions but *our* questions. They are, in short, inescapably *public* questions about how we are going to continue to live together in this representative democracy—if we are.

The introduction is about writing and reading books such as this. It is cast as a piece of a memoir and is intended to be somewhat whimsical. But I intend it also to be an argument for exploring the possibility of turning a *Kulturkampf* into a civil conversation. Chapters one and two are about the limits and imperatives of the political, with special reference to the priority of the cultural. There I try to explain why we today tend to take politics too seriously, and not seriously enough. The third chapter is "Remembering the Movement," an effort to understand the 1960s as a moment of moral luminosity and as a moral slum of a decade. The fourth and fifth chapters go together, although it may seem their subjects have little to do with each other. One is about the underclass, mainly the black underclass, in our cities. The other is about the people who rescued Jews during the Holocaust. As I say, they are about the same thing. Some readers may be tempted to skip the sixth and seventh chapters, but I earnestly hope they resist. The subject is the abortion debate, and how the abortion debate is about ever so much more than abortion, and why—no matter how much we might wish it otherwise—there is no going around that debate if we are to understand "America against itself." The final chapter is, as final chapters ought to be, the conclusion. Not a conclusion supplying satisfactory answers to all the questions raised, to be sure. But there are conclusions in the final chapter. Among the most important is that our peculiarly American discussion of who we are and who we ought to be assumes that the discussion will not be brought to a conclusion.

I am asked whether this book is optimistic or pessimistic about the American experiment. I trust it is neither. Optimism and pessimism are merely selective ways of looking at things, blocking out what we are determined not to see. I intend these pages to be sober and sobering, yet hopeful and, just maybe, hope instilling. We do not need to know how the American experiment is going to turn out, or even what it means to say that it might turn out this way or that. All that follows in this book is informed by a metaphysical lightheartedness that some call faith. I take it that that is what Eliot meant when he wrote, "For us, there is only the trying. The rest is not our business."

I am especially indebted to James Nuechterlein, editor of *First Things: A Monthly Journal of Religion and Public Life,* for reading the manuscript with care and offering important suggestions. Also to the staff of the Institute on Religion and Public Life, especially Davida Goldman and Paul Stallsworth, and Matthew Berke. My thanks, once again, to the Community of Christ in the City, with whom I live and by whom I am nourished in body and spirit.

I will say no more here about the writing of this book. That is what the introduction is about. Well, perhaps only this: In the preface to one of his books, Reinhold Niebuhr asked the reader to keep in mind that he is most critical of the proclivities of others to which he is himself most prone. That applies to this author as well.

RJN

Epiphany, 1992
New York City

Introduction
The Continuing Conversation

Karl Kraus, that prolific Viennese writer at the turn of the century, was once asked by a student, "Herr Professor Kraus, why do you write books?" Kraus answered, "Because, young man, I have not character enough not to." That is not the whole story about writing books, but I suspect it is an important part of it.

When I was about nine years old somebody gave me one of those purple gelatin mixtures you put into a baking pan. I think it was called hectographing, but older readers will know what I mean. By rubbing sheets of paper against the impression on the gelatin I could produce about thirty legible copies, which was just right for the circulation of a really first-class neighborhood newspaper for Miller Street in Pembroke, Ontario. So you can see that from early on my lack of character was such that I assumed people would be, or should be, interested in what I had to say. There was recently an item in the *New York Times* indicating that an alarming percentage of today's writers started out as children producing neighborhood newspapers. Parents should take note. By nipping the habit in the bud they are perhaps in the best position to alleviate the glut of writing that is presently stifling what remains of Western civilization.

Because nobody caught me in time—and some adults who should have known better actually encouraged me—it has been downhill from the Miller Street Gazette. During

1

a brief stay at Concordia High School in Seward, Nebraska, I wrote for the student newspaper. (The president of the school had the good judgment to let me know that my career probably lay elsewhere than at Concordia, so I never did finish high school, moving directly on to college and other phases of what we persist in calling higher education.) At Seward, I wrote a piece that particularly excited me on the operation of Concordia's cafeteria. Tough investigative reporting turned up, among other things, the information that something like two thousand loaves of bread were baked there each week. It was not that anyone was trying to conceal the fact, but neither was anyone paying much attention to it, and I thought they should.

It was later, as an editor of *The Seminarian* at Concordia Seminary, St. Louis, that the vice of writing was exercised on weightier matters—such as the chronology of Genesis, the historicity of the Resurrection, and why it was all right for Catholics and Protestants to pray together. We're talking about the late 1950s when the church of which Concordia Seminary was part was churning with controversies beyond numbering. *The Seminarian* was the favored foil of the seminary's conservative critics. The administration pooh-poohed our literary excursions into heresy (meaning anything beyond the bounds of what the church in solemn assembly defined as true), pointing out that kids will be kids. But the critics knew better. If you don't stop them now, these kids might later start writing books that at least some innocent readers would take seriously. What the critics didn't know is that, in my case, it was already about fifteen years too late. The time for corrective action was with the first issue of the Miller Street Gazette. "Train a child in the way he should go. . . ."

Later—some fourteen books, hundreds of articles, and innumerable columns and reviews later—the toll taken on the minds and patience of readers is unconscionable. Karl Kraus's answer to the student was, I believe, astute. I am frequently asked by young people who take me to be a writer how one becomes a writer. As though it were similar to becoming a gynecologist or academic dean. My impulse, seldom restrained, is to say that, if you aren't a writer already, don't bother. A writer writes and writes and keeps on writing, and then some day some people may take him to be a writer. And, if he is never publicly recognized as such, he must then decide whether he will write as a solitary vice. Maybe posterity will discover him, although posterity is as unperceptive as anyone else. I do not say that writers are born rather than made. But, if they are not born, they are at least bent at an early age.

There is the opinion that a prerequisite to becoming a writer is to believe that you have something to say. That strikes me as only partly true. I would not know that I have something to say were it not for the things being said by others that should not be said, or that are in urgent need of correction. Meaning no offense, and perhaps agreeing with the reader who has just come to the idea while reading this, so much foolishness is published these days. Being an incorrigible reader, three times a day I stumble across something I want to counter with an article, and at least once a day across something that calls for a book in refutation. I do restrain myself, however. I wait a decent interval for someone else to do the needed correcting but, if that is not forthcoming, I, with keyboard and a little time at hand, do my duty.

I know an eminent and prolific writer who claims that he has never written anything except he was asked to write it by someone else. Such laissez-faire devotion to the publishing market—supplying only what is demanded—is impressive, but quite beyond my ken. As best I can remember, nobody asked for the Miller Street Gazette. I do not suggest that all my writing is reactive, provoked by the silly things written by others, which it is my duty to set straight. You cannot be forever correcting arguments that other people got all wrong without somebody, sooner or late, challenging you to make the argument the way it should be made. From the imprudence of responding to that challenge come books and, in the words of Martin Luther's *Small Catechism*, "other great shame and vice." Luther, some would suggest, learned the hard way.

There is the perennial talk about "publish or perish" in the professorial world, and, acting on that imperative, legions of academics have published and perished. We are told about these assistant professors who publish because they are hungry for tenure or eager to advance their discipline, or both. These people no doubt exist, but my hunch is that publication is more commonly prompted by wanting to straighten out some dumb thing published by somebody else. There are other purposes in writing. There is, for instance, the satisfaction of seeing one's name in print, especially on a book jacket. As for politicians "to be on TV is to be," so for the writer a book is the visible and outward sign of the spiritual and inward conviction that one is a writer. But, chiefly, I expect it is the case that writers *like* to write. I have writer friends who regale me with tales of the sheer anguish they go through in writing. But write they do. If they were really masochistic personalities, it would likely show up in other ways as well, but it doesn't. I think they love it. Maybe they talk about the anguish to assuage their guilt over getting so much satisfaction from something so self-indulgent as writing.

Not that the above is not serious, but more seriously: If we must talk about a purpose in writing, it is in continuing a conversation. The conversation has been going on for many centuries, and maybe it will continue for many centuries more. This lifetime is our little moment to keep it going. The thought is exhilarating, humbling, and sometimes just wearying. Over the years I have been, *inter alia*, book editor for several journals. I recall one bright afternoon talking with a visitor at my office, then on East 64th Street in Manhattan. The office was crowded with hundreds of books received for review. There they were, piles and piles of them, awaiting judgment according to the editorial triage system—review, briefly note, toss.

And what are you working on now? my visitor asked. Well, I'm working on this book about. . . . And then I stopped, struck by the improbability of the world really needing another book, never mind another book by me. When it comes to the making of books, the writer of Ecclesiastes didn't know the half of it. Last year there were over 70,000 trade books published in the United States alone. That does not include specialized scholarly books, nor at least as many volumes put out by institutes, corporations, and government agencies. Even if he sticks to his own field, anyone who today says that he is "on top of the literature" is probably perched atop a very high stack of unread books.

Young people who want to be writers should know that, with a relatively minuscule number of exceptions, nobody makes a living at this business. Other than novels, a serious book today—which is to say any book that requires what used to be a twelfth-grade level of literacy—does well to sell 5,000 copies and is a best seller at 15,000. Beyond that it is a sensation. Multiply the number sold by the cover price of the book, and calculate that the author gets 10 or 15 percent. It readily becomes apparent why writing books is for people who, if not of independent means, have an honest job.

John Locke got all sorts of things wrong, but he knew about books. "Books seem to me," he wrote, "to be pestilent things, and infect all that trade in them with something very perverse and brutal. Printers, binders, sellers, and others that make a trade and gain out of them have universally so odd a turn and corruption of mind that they have a way of dealing peculiar to themselves, and not conformed to the good of society and that general fairness which cements mankind."

It might all be very depressing, were it not for this business about the continuing conversation. Rather, the many continuing conversations, the most engaging and important of which, many of us think, is that of the community of reflective faith. In writing, it perhaps helps if one is something of a preacher. The preacher has no illusions about the novelty of what he has to say. Not novelty but fidelity is his business. Although, to be sure, he tries to transmit the faith in ways that are fresh, if not new. Mankind, said Dr. Johnson, has a greater need to be reminded than to be instructed. Nor does the preacher have any illusions about being able to demonstrate the effectiveness of his efforts. A long time ago, when I was young and brash, I thought that Isaiah's promise that "the word will not return void" (Isaiah 55) was the consolation of incompetent preachers. Many years later I know better, or maybe I just know that we incompetents can't get along without our consolations. So also in writing: you do not know what effect your words may have. If the book is read beyond the circle of obliging friends and relatives, you do not even know the partners in the conversation.

An acquaintance of mine (not a friend; I do not think he reads my books) announced upon sending another scholarly tome off to the publisher, "It is like dropping a very beautiful rose petal down a very deep well, never to be heard from again." He claims that Calvin said something similar about doomed souls. A friend (he does read my books) who is a philosopher has a quite different view. He is utterly confident of the place of his work in the history of ideas. No future laborer in the philosophical vineyard, he is convinced, will be able to go around what he has contributed to the conversation. Because this friend is a genius of monumental stature, I am not inclined to argue.

Most of us, however, are somewhere between the deep-well theory and being sure about our place in the world-historical scheme of things. And some people appear to have given up thinking about it and, or so it seems, just publish to be publishing. One writer (who consistently finds it worthwhile to review my books only in order to announce that this one, too, is not worth reading) published so many books that it was said he had no unpublished thoughts. Then he published a torrid book on sexuality, after which it was said that he had no unpublished fantasies.

Such abandonment of restraint suggests a paraphrase of that ugly sentiment espoused by some soldiers of fortune: Publish them all and let God sort them out.

But that is not the kind of conversation I have in mind when I speak of the continuing conversation. Real conversation has to do with discrete traditions; it has to do with the kind of thing that Jaroslav Pelikan describes in his admirable *The Vindication of Tradition*.[1] Pelikan writes about the importance of the "florilegium," the work of Eastern Orthodox scribes who wrote history by stringing together quotations from earlier writers. The originality of the florilegium was not in anything that was said directly but in the originality of the way the tradition was arranged. I take it that that is what Dr. Johnson meant by the importance of being reminded.

All of us who write should keep the idea of the florilegium at least somewhere in mind. Otherwise we are just putting ourselves forward or, as they say, "expressing" ourselves. And that is not too different from putting out the Miller Street Gazette. This book aspires to being something more than that.

1. The Modesty
of the Political

I never know quite what to make of the claim that a college generation consists of four years, at most. One hears it from college teachers who seem to be excusing the *ad hoc* nature of education divorced from the continuities of tradition. One hears it also from other teachers who are not interested in excuses but are keenly aware of how little can be taken for granted when it comes to shared points of reference, to common knowledge and common experience. They complain that our culture is obsessed with the new and the immediate, and there is no doubt much justice in that complaint. And of course there are those for whom it is not a complaint but an ideological campaign against any suggestion that there are normative traditions or authoritative precedents. The campaign sometimes takes the form of an all-out "war against the canon." As the picketers at Stanford University put it a couple of years ago, "Hey, hey, ho, ho, Western civ got to go!" Why should the present defer to the past? they in the radical mode ask. Why indeed? The truth is that we are by now so familiar with such demands of the Imperious Now that they no longer seem radical at all.

One suspects that there are other people, including students, who have had their fill of being told that we live in a time of unprecedented rapidity of change, that the past is deserving of dismissal as *mere* prelude, that our brief moment on the stage of history is what the whole of the

9

human story has been working itself up to until now, and so forth. When we begin to doubt these cliches of an importunate presentism, however, another uneasiness sets in. Not with everybody, but with many people, the uneasiness comes from the suspicion that one may be in the process of becoming conservative. Whether or not that suspicion causes uneasiness depends in large part upon one's prior experience with conservatism. Just as there are varieties of radicalism and varieties of liberalism, so also there are at least as many varieties of conservatism. They range from the grotesque to the winsome, from the fantastic to the plausible, from the clamorous to the consoling.

At present, many more Americans say they are conservative than say they are liberal, and the conservative imbalance is even more striking among young people. It is hard to know what that means, however. In the context of the polling business, "conservative" and "liberal" are usually defined by the political issues that are current. It is quite predictable that at some point in the future the majority of people will once again describe themselves as liberal. The pundits will hail that as a very big change, but it may not be much of a change at all. Everything depends upon which issues, memories, sensibilities, fears and aspirations are then being packed into the political travel bags labeled "conservative" and "liberal."

While today it is said that a conservative "mood" is regnant in our culture, it is certainly not evident in all parts of the culture. Except for writers and publications clearly identified as conservative, American intellectual life, and especially academic life, is emphatically liberal. This is true as well of the prestige communications media and of the major foundations that are so important to the funding of research and public argument. To take note of this liberal predominance is not to issue a charge or complaint. It is the way things are. Every six months or so we get another study demonstrating definitively that 70 or 80 percent of leaders in the media or in selected fields of academe are substantially to the left on the liberal-conservative spectrum. That has been the case for decades and will likely continue to be the case.

There are many reasons why this should be the way things are. In recent years, this state of affairs has been explained by some in terms of "new class theory."[1] The details of that theory need not detain us here. Suffice it that there is considerable persuasive force in the proposal that there is an identifiable new class or "knowledge class" that, like other classes, has its own class interests. In this case, the distinctive interest is in the production and distribution of ideas, and in expanding the governmental power by which those ideas can be implemented in society. The goal, of course, is a better and more just society—or at least what members of the new class think to be a better and more just society. New class theory has an important measure of explanatory value. But there are other, and perhaps less polemical, ways of thinking about the dominance of liberalism in elite sectors of the culture.

Numerous scholars have made the argument that all of American thought—at least all of it that is identifiably *American*—is liberal. Even conservatives, in this view, are really conservative liberals. Conservativisms are variations on a liberal theme, so to speak. This argument emphasizes that identifiably American thought is built on foundations such as those laid by John Locke, Adam Smith, Thomas Jefferson, and John Stuart Mill. All these worthies are liberals or the precursors of modern liberalism because of their accent on the individual, the role of reason, limited government, historical progress, tolerance, and the free market of ideas. They are generally cool toward the notion of authoritative tradition, especially religious tradition, and tend to favor the privatization of the big questions about the meaning of life and death.

That, in strokes admittedly broad, is what people mean by liberalism when they say that the entirety of our cultural tradition is liberal. This can lead to curiosities in the way we think about liberal and conservative. For instance, those who call themselves libertarians today are commonly counted among political conservatives. Libertarians, however, favor a thoroughly stripped-down government in order to maximize the sphere of individual freedom, and might more accurately be called extreme (they would say more consistent) liberals. Similarly, those who have been called neoconservatives in the last two decades are typically insistent that they are the true liberals. For that reason, some of them prefer to call themselves neoliberals. In any event, neoconservatives understand themselves to be contending for the liberal tradition and against restrictive measures that are currently proposed in the name of liberalism. Cases in point are racial quotas, policies aimed at "equality of result" rather than "equality of opportunity," and ideological tests (often feminist or Marxist) in academic appointments.

Gilbert's doggerel in *Iolanthe* would seem to be to the point: "I often think it's comical/ How nature always does contrive/ That every boy and every gal,/ That's born into the world alive,/ Is either a little Liberal,/ Or else a little Conservative!" But that was a century ago in England. In our cultural and political situation it seems to be getting harder to tell who is a little liberal and who is a little conservative, or when one is being a little of either. Consider, for instance, the public debate over abortion policy. In the way it has been played out in the political arena, it is assumed that the "prochoice" position is liberal and the "prolife" position is conservative. There are those who would make the case, however, that the prolife position better accords with that dimension of liberalism that urges upon us a more inclusive definition of the human community for which we accept common responsibility. Or consider the Christian fundamentalists who agitate for the right to educate their children according to their own beliefs, free from government interference. Such people are conventionally viewed as being on the far right edge of conservatism, and yet we must at least entertain the counterview that their insistence on the "free exercise of religion" is at the heart of the liberal tradition.

In present disputes, quite contradictory arguments are advanced, often by the same people and at the same time. For example, liberals tell us that, on issues such as capital punishment, conservatives are long on justice but short on compassion. When it comes to "systemic change of unjust social structures," however, the same people tell us that conservatives are long on compassion but short on justice, since conservatives favor philanthropic help for the poor but oppose changing the system that, it is said, makes people poor. Turnabout seems to be fair play, also in the making of contradictory arguments. So conservatives regularly accuse liberals of being long on abstract principles but out of touch with the common sense and feelings of ordinary people. In the same breath, liberals are accused of abandoning absolute truths in their infinitely flexible and complexifying compulsion to "respond to the needs of real people." In these and many other ways, the polemics between liberals and conservatives, between right and left, drive a linguistic spiral descending into an ever deeper muddle.

Some people are so conservative, a favorite uncle of mine remarked, that, had they been asked on the first day of creation, they would have voted for chaos. To which my conservative aunt responded that some people are so liberal that they think the expulsion from the garden was a great blow for freedom. The argument went downhill from there, and that was some thirty years ago. The dispute is no more elevated today. It is little wonder that many people throw up their hands in disgust and say that we should forget altogether about labels such as conservative and liberal. "Just say what you have to say, and never mind putting a political or ideological adjective on it." That is a very attractive proposal and should not be dismissed lightly. Thank goodness, many of the most important things that we each have to say cannot be fitted into the thought-slots of the political spectrum. Beginning with, for example, "I love you." Those who insist upon knowing whether that is a liberal or a conservative statement are, after a while, not likely to hear it very often.

One of the most important contributions of religious folk is to challenge the imperiousness of the political, along with all its pomps and pretensions and divisive labels. At least religious folk *should* so challenge the imperiousness of the political. Biblical religion opens us to the worlds beyond and within the everyday reality that we call the world. In this awakened consciousness, all worldly contests of power are sharply relativized, their inflated pretensions to importance debunked. "He who sits in the heavens laughs; the Lord has them in derision" (Psalm 2). He laughs not because he does not care, but because he cares so much about his children who so pitiably got it all wrong. What we in our conspiring and plotting and taking counsel together think is happening is not what is happening at all.

"I beseech you, in the bowels of Christ, think it possible you may be mistaken," Oliver Cromwell wrote in 1650 to ecclesiastics who had an unseemly confidence in their own grasp of the truth. It would not be long before others would be directing the same plea to Cromwell who, as Lord Protector, betrayed an overweening certitude about his perception of God's purposes. It is a plea that faithful Christians and Jews should direct to all political rulers and would-be rulers. But, before they can do that very convincingly, they need to direct that plea to one another.

Back in "*the* movement" of the 1960s, it was commonly said, "If you're not part of the solution, you're part of the problem." The churches today, it is to be feared, are part of the problem of the imperiousness of the political. That is to say, the great political and ideological divides in our society are not challenged by the churches but run right through the churches, and are thus reinforced by the churches. It is no exaggeration to say that our society is embroiled in a

Kulturkampf, a war over the meaning of American culture. In ways sometimes maddeningly confused, the battle lines follow the distinctions between liberal and conservative, right and left. In terms of both general disposition and specific issues, most of us can, with appropriate qualifications, locate ourselves, or at least pieces of ourselves, on the battle map. But there precisely is the problem. We are not content to have a piece of ourselves here and a piece of ourselves there. We want a place where *we* can stand with integrity, instead of parceling ourselves out in pieces to one side or another. Communities of religious faith ought to provide such a place. The designation— the label, if you will— of "Christian" ought to have definitional priority in describing who we are and intend to be. The same is true of Jews who are Jews not by the accidents of Jewishness but by adherence to the truth of Judaism.

Religious communities should strive to be a zone of truth in a world of politicized mendacity. The objection is immediately raised that surely it is unfair to the political enterprise to say that it is, of necessity, mendacious. The objection does not survive careful examination, and we will be coming back to such examination in the chapters that follow. Suffice it that politics is, among other things, about the getting and keeping of power. And power, to put it bluntly, is the capacity to persuade or compel others to do what you want. To be sure, that is not all that politics is. And, to be sure again, honorable people in politics only want other people to do what they believe they should do in order to serve the common good. But in a free society there are, and should be, different visions of the common good. Therefore, there are and should be parties, alliances, and coalitions for action. And, like it or not, all parties, alliances, and coalitions for action are defined in distinction from, and of necessity against, other parties, alliances, and coalitions for action. Of course, each group is tempted to think that it has a monopoly on concern for the common good and is only against other groups because they are indifferent or hostile to the common good. That is a temptation and a conceit that is to be resisted, and believers should be in the vanguard of the resistance.

Even when that temptation is successfully resisted, the political actor is still engaged in mendacity. That is not necessarily a moral fault. It is the nature of the political game. The reference to "game" is instructive. In football, the quarterback is under no obligation to signal his plays to the opposing team. On the contrary, his purpose is to conceal and, if possible, mislead. Lest I be misunderstood as endorsing cynicism about politics, I quickly add that some of my good (if not best) friends over the years have been politicians. And some of them protest publicly, and even privately, that they have not a thought in their heads other than to do the right thing in order to serve the common good. A capacity for searching introspection is not usually considered a political asset. But more reflective politicians know that doing "the right thing" has many parts. One part is staying in office so that one can continue to do the right thing in the future. Another part is getting one's fellow (and sister) politicians to do the right thing, too.

Not everyone agrees on what is the right thing with respect to everything. Nor, even when they agree on the right thing with respect to this or that, do politicians rank this or that in the same order of importance. So the effective politician learns to exchange another's service to his right thing for his service to another's right thing, in the hope that it all ends up serving the common good. Thus are alliances, always more or less provisional, formed. All the while, other politicians are doing what they believe is the right thing that our politician is convinced is the wrong thing. Only on editorial pages and in the sermons of political preachers (the two often being hard to tell apart) do all right things converge in the doing of *the* right thing, which of course is what the editorialist or preacher thinks to be the right thing.

So far we have been assuming a measure of moral integrity on the part of all the actors involved. That is not a safe assumption. Not only must politicians conceal, mislead, and tailor the truth so that it becomes, for the purposes at hand, a *useful* truth, but they must also work with those to whom right and truth have little meaning. One might argue that Pontius Pilate was an effective politician, and he perhaps should not be blamed for the one decision that could not be contained within his framework of political prudence.

In speaking about politics and mendacity, I do not wish to offend devout believers in Washington or in state houses and city halls across the country. I have written elsewhere about politics as a worthy vocation for Christians.[2] The point here is merely to second Reinhold Niebuhr's magisterially detailed analysis of politics as an enterprise of inherent moral ambiguity. Morally reflective politicians do not need to read Niebuhr to be persuaded of that ambiguity. Precisely because they know something of the mendacity of the political, they are the first to agree on the necessity of maintaining the limits of the political. I am struck by the fact that Christian politicians are usually in ready agreement that the church should strive to be a zone of truth, to maintain a measure of immunity and distance from partisan contestations. Political activists in the churches, those who would extend the political arena of the civil realm into the life of the church, say they are not surprised that professional politicians feel that way. Such politicians, it is claimed, simply want to be protected from the "prophetic" witness of the churches. I expect that is both inaccurate and unfair to the politicians in question. They know something about the corrupting dynamics of the political and would like to see some sectors of society, notably the churches, provide an antidote, or at least a contrast, to those dynamics.

In *The Restructuring of American Religion*, Robert Wuthnow of Princeton has produced convincing evidence that the churches are less and less providing a "contrast institution" by which political and other enterprises can be critically assessed.[3] In some respects, there is not much that is new in this finding. H. Richard Niebuhr, for example, taught an earlier generation to recognize "the social sources of denominationalism."[4] While denominations explained their existence in terms of distinctive theological or spiritual claims, Niebuhr argued, they more often than not were started and sustained by "social sources," such as ethnicity, language, and class. Nobody should want to deny the unremitting humanness of the churches that constitute the Christian community. Nobody familiar with the institutional machinations within our churches needs to take lessons from politicians when it comes to the human capacity for mendacity. Such dynamics are the more lethal in the church when they are disguised in the treacle of piety and cloying claims of unalloyed devotion to the will of God. All that said, churches are nonetheless structured by different ordering truths, or at least they profess to be.

Theological truth claims and professed fidelity to the God of Abraham, Isaac, Jacob, and Jesus should make a difference. Our faith communities should not be religious appendages to the ideological and political options that are in play in the civil realm. Agreement on this point can by no means be taken for granted today. So far advanced is the politicizing of our churches that those who raise a question about it are charged with being unhappy only because it is not *their* politics that the church is promoting. If the church in question is fundamentalist and is allied with others in "returning America to Bible law," criticism of that course is interpreted as a willingness to compromise and raises suspicions of "spineless liberalism." If the church in question is left-of-center on the political spectrum, critics are dismissed as cranky conservatives who would not be complaining if the church were promoting the politics that they favor.

In some circles one encounters a "free church" view-point run amuck. The message, in effect, is this: "If you don't like the politics of Grace Episcopal, go join Calvary Temple where they push the politics you prefer." First decide about your politics, and then choose a church to fit your political proclivities. One encounters people who see no problem with that. An argument of this book is that it is a very big problem. It is the problem, not to put too fine a point on it, of apostasy from the constituting truth claims of Christianity.

In saying that the church should challenge and relativize the imperiousness of the political, the point is not that the church has no interest in the political. On the contrary, it is precisely and critically a *political* contribution of the church to liberate us from the pretensions of the political. Anabaptist theologian Vernard Eller has very provocatively made that case in *Christian Anarchy: Jesus' Primacy Over the Powers*.[5] Eller is no doubt too provocative for many. "Anarchy" is not the alternative to politicized religion that most of us seek. We might want to claim a measure of dignity for the political task, even to say that it participates in the divinely instituted "orders of preservation." But, given the politically diseased state of American Christianity, Eller's argument is a salutary antidote to be taken in regular doses. No doubt there are those who will resist the prescription, fearing that it could revive the axiom that "religion and politics don't mix"—an axiom ever odious to liberal Christians, and one in which conservative Christians, for the most part, no longer believe.

Oddly enough, a robust skepticism toward the political, an insistence that politics stay in its place, can actually elevate the dignity of politics. What is politics, after all? It includes, to be sure, the less edifying dynamics mentioned above. But politics at its heart, Aristotle said, is insepa-rable from ethics. Politics, he argued, is the activity of free persons (he said free men, of course) deliberating the question of how they ought to order their life together in relation to the good. It is doubtful that anybody has come up with a better short statement of what politics is, or should be. The use of "ought" and the reference to "the good" make it inescapably clear that politics is a moral enterprise. Of course it is not a moral enterprise in the sense that those who practice it always behave morally. It is moral in the sense that it engages the questions of right and wrong, of good and evil. Many political decisions are purely instrumental in nature: What's the best way of getting to an agreed upon goal? But other decisions are unavoidably moral in nature and, if we scratch the supposedly instrumental decisions, we discover that they too are often premised upon unexamined moral assumptions.

Politics as a moral enterprise participates in, but can never be permitted to subsume, our understanding of the moral. Neither, for that matter, can the moral be permitted to subsume the entirety of our lives. The "three transcendents" are the good, the true, and the beautiful. The other two cannot be collapsed into the good, just as the good must not be collapsed into the political. Politics, understood at its most elevated level, is a subspecies of the good. It can participate in, but it cannot comprehend, *the* good of human life. That good is perfect communion with the Absolute Good, who is God. Or, as the Shorter Catechism of Westminster (1647) puts it, "Man's chief end is to glorify God and to enjoy Him forever." Aristotle's politics is the right ordering of our life together short of that chief end. What today is usually meant by "politics" is less than that. For most of us, and it should be the case for all of us, the most important dimensions of "our life together" have little to do with what is ordinarily meant by politics.

It seems odd that politics should be elevated by being reduced, but so it is. Why this is so is not hard to discover. If politics encompasses the entirety of existence and defines *the* good of our lives, then politics is a false god that biblical believers must repudiate without reservation. In the biblical scheme of things, *the* right ordering of our lives was fatally disrupted on that unfortunate afternoon in the Garden of Eden and will not be fully restored until the Messianic Age. In the light of Augustine's amendment of Aristotle, it is understood that the only *polis* deserving of our ultimate devotion is the City of God. Our devotion to the right ordering of the earthly *polis* is penultimate and, in most of its aspects, prepenultimate. Our engagement in the politics of the earthly city is guided by God's backstop, for-the-time-being, emergency ordinances that he mercifully instituted in order to see us through until his original right ordering is restored in the coming of the Kingdom.

Christians consider that the church is the community in which the right ordering of that coming Kingdom is proclaimed, celebrated, and anticipated by faith. To the extent that they live as Christ's disciples in relation to one another, that right ordering is exemplified by their life together in the church, although always in a manner that is painfully inadequate. The church is brought into being and is sustained by the Living Word. The faith of Christians is not in the manner of their celebrating, nor in the sincerity of their faith, nor in the quality of their discipleship, but in the Word. And the Word is not only the word about the Kingdom but is the Word who is Christ the King. Gathered by that Word around that Word, Christians understand themselves to be engaged in the politics of the right ordering of human life together. Any politics that refuses to be humbled by *that* politics is to be recognized and named as the politics of the Evil One. Without going into detail here, it can be readily demonstrated that there are closely cognate understandings of law, covenant, peoplehood, and universal promise in Judaism.[6]

When it has been duly humbled and has abandoned its overweening pretensions to supreme importance, politics can be elevated by admission to the life of the community of faith. It can be admitted on the same basis as any other legitimate concern that some believers are called to pursue. The vocation of the community is to sustain many vocations, and the political vocation is one among the many. It is by no means the most important. Nor, thank God, are most members of the community called to it, although in a democracy such as ours nobody should neglect the minimal responsibilities of citizenship. (One does not wish to be legalistic about this. The person who does not vote because "it only encourages them" may think he is exercising his responsibility as a citizen, although we may be permitted to disagree.) Within the context of all the worlds invoked by the good, the true, and the beautiful, we can affirm the calling of those who attend to the modest world of politics.

Judges 9 may be instructive in this connection. Recall wicked Abimelech at Shechem who slew his brothers, save one, and had himself made king. Jotham, the surviving brother, stood on the top of Mount Gerizim and shouted a parable to the Shechemites. In this parable, the trees, looking for a king to rule over them, first offered the throne to the olive tree. But the olive tree said, "Shall I leave my fatness, by which gods and men are honored, and go to sway over the trees?" Next they went to the fig tree, but the fig tree said that producing its "sweetness and good fruit" was more important than ruling. Then they went to the grape vine and said, "Come and reign over us." But the vine said, "Shall I leave my wine which cheers gods and men, and go to sway over the trees?" Finally, in desperation, the trees offered the throne to the bramble bush. The bramble, not having much else to do of importance, consented. It may not be the moral intended by the inspired writer of Judges, but one may infer from the parable a useful point about the modesty of the political task.

The present writer and perhaps most who read this book share in the calling to the political task, at least to the extent of trying to understand the connections between faith and the public order. No doubt there will be some readers who have what is called a full-time vocation to politics. Others have the responsibility of formulating programs, or teaching courses, or taking courses, related to religion, morality, and politics. Whether the political dimension is major or minor in our vocations, we will all do our work much better if we understand that we are not doing the most important thing in the world. It may be the most important thing for *us* to do because it is what we believe we are called to do, but not because it is the most important thing in the world. Our pride may be offended by the thought that God would call us to do something less than the most important thing in the world, but so it is. My firm intuition is that, in the judgment of God and of the innumerable angels watching from the celestial galleries, a priest speaking the word of forgiveness to a despairing sinner, a volunteer anointing the sores of one afflicted with AIDS, a wife praying for the strength to stick by her drunken husband, and a violinist playing Bach's Concerto in A minor are all probably doing something much more important than whatever the president of the United States is doing at this moment. If we are not at least open to that possibility, our world is much too small.

Here is Leo the Great (d. 461), preaching to the Christians in Rome: "Touch physical light with the bodily sense and embrace with all the power of your soul that true light 'that enlightens every man coming into the world,' of which the prophet says, 'Look on him, and be radiant; so your faces shall never be ashamed.' For if we are the temple of God and the Spirit of God dwells within us, what each of the faithful has in his soul is greater than what can be seen in the heavens." If greater than what can be seen in the heavens, how much greater still than what can be done on Capitol Hill or read about in tomorrow's newspaper.

Nonetheless. We should try to do well what we have been given to do, even if it is not so important in the cosmic scheme of things. And so those of us to whom it is given to think about politics return to the disputes over the meanings of liberal and conservative and similar questions that bear upon the right ordering of our life together in this provisional period prior to *the* right ordering of our life together. In the next chapter we consider alternative, and sometimes conflicting, ways of thinking about politics—ways that derive from presuppositions proposed here. Then we move on to a somewhat more autobiographical discussion. It is a reflection on the notorious or celebrated (take your pick) 1960s, and how our present political alignments, and divisions, came about. It is a reflection on being radical, which I take to be another word for being faithful to the good, even to the Ultimate Good.

2. Politics and the Best Thing In the World

The beginning of political wisdom is to recognize both the importance and the limits of the political. That, in turn, requires that we recognize the importance and the limits of humanity. "Were man the best thing in the world," says Aristotle, "political science and prudence would be the most perfect knowledge; but the most perfect knowledge is rather of the highest objects—of the highest objects, we say; for it would be strange to think that the art of politics, or practical wisdom, is the best knowledge, since man is not the best thing in the world" (*Ethics* VI). According to Aristotle, the contemplative life is superior to the political life because it participates in the self-dependent actuality of thought, which is life, which is God most good and eternal (*Metaphysics* XII).

This asserted distinction between the contemplative and the political, the eternal and the temporal, the higher and the lower, the sacred and the profane is unpalatable to many of our contemporaries. It reflects a "classical tradition" which speaks of the transcendent—a way of speaking we have presumably transcended. With significant variations, it also reflects a "religious worldview" of Augustine, Maimonides, Aquinas, Luther, and Calvin which is, we are told, no longer believable. Those who advance such worldviews are accused of trying to drag us back into a necessarily discarded past of pre-scientific irrationality. According to the intellectual orthodoxy of our time, man is not only the best thing in the world, man is the only thing in the world—or at least the only thing that can bestow meaning upon the world, and upon our selves in the world.

Those who are set against the proposition are not likely to be persuaded in these few pages that politics is not properly understood apart from metaphysics, or that the modern state is in important respects a religious phenomenon produced by a putatively secular age. But I invite the reader to be at least open to entertaining such ideas, for such ideas underlie the argument that we are presently experiencing a crisis in democratic theory and practice—and this at a time when, after the Revolution of 1989 in Eastern Europe, almost the entire world is declaring its enthusiasm for democracy.

The argument here assumes that there are important *distinctions* to be made between politics, ethics, and metaphysics. Politics has to do with the ordering of relationships between free actors, subject to the ruling principle of reason and in service to justice by which respective rights and duties are determined. Such a formulation is heavily freighted with concepts such as freedom, reason, justice, rights, and duties. The meaning of none of them is self-evident. Many contemporary political thinkers claim that some or all of them are, in fact, meaningless. We are told that discourse about such concepts only obfuscates clear analysis of what politics actually *is* in the real world.

The political question, it is said, is not, as Aristotle thought, How ought we to order our life together? The political question is how, in the real world, power is acquired and maintained and lost. On this view, political theory and practice do not require an account of "the good." And that is thought to be a very good thing because no account of the good is available to us—or at least no account of the good on which we can achieve anything like a consensus. This way of thinking about politics not only accepts, but insists upon, a sharp distinction, even a divorce, between "fact" and "value." Political thought, if it is to be scientific, must attend to the facts. It must refuse to enter into discussion of values, except as values can be treated as facts of human valuing. Otherwise, we are warned, the discussion of values may slide into the discussion of moral facts (an intolerable oxymoron), or even of religion.

In *The Myth of the State*, Ernst Cassirer describes the strangeness of modern politics.

> The modern politicians have had to solve a problem that in many respects resembles squaring the circle. The historians of human civilization have told us that mankind in its development had to pass through two different phases. Man began as a *homo magus* ; but from the age of magic he passed to the age of technics. The *homo magus* of former times and primitive civilization became a *homo faber*, a craftsman and artisan. If we admit such an historical distinction our modern political myths appear indeed as a very strange and paradoxical thing. For what we find in them is the blending of two activities that seem to exclude each other. The modern politician has had to combine in himself two entirely different and even incompatible functions. He has to act, at the same time, as both a *homo magus* and a *homo faber*. *He is the priest of a new, entirely irrational and mysterious religion.*[1]

It is as though, paraphrasing Oscar Wilde, politics has become the religion that dare not speak its name. And, lest it be tempted to come out of the closet, so to speak, it must be rigorously segregated from forms of religion that do declare themselves to be religion.

The history of modern thought, including political thought, has been a determined turn toward the subject, a turn toward ourselves. Augustine declared that the human heart is restless until it rests in the best, who is God. Agreeing with Augustine on the restlessness, but finding God unavailable, human beings have declared themselves to be the best thing in the world. This radical turn, *mutatis mutandis*, is evident in the arguments advanced from

Machiavelli through Hobbes, Locke, Rousseau, Hume, Bentham, Mill, Feuerbach, and Marx. Humanity is one with, and is exhausted by, Nature; we are explained by, and all our explanations are functions of, Nature. The apotheosis of this way of thinking is reached in Marx's "generic man," in which all alienations are overcome between Man, Nature, and History. The gap between the "is" and the "ought" is bridged, and immortality is achieved in the revelation that God *is* Man. In that eschatological fulfillment, religion, which is the sigh of an oppressed humanity, is finally superseded and all tensions between the sacred and the profane, between the "now" and "not yet," are resolved.

Those who are viewed as conservative thinkers in our day do not need to be warned against the dangers of such as Feuerbach or Marx. Conservative heroes such as Adam Smith and Edmund Burke, however, often seem to be not so different from their supposed ideological opposites in dealing with the question at hand. At least for purposes of political theory, they too are interpreted as suggesting that humanity is the best, indeed the only, thing in the world. In Burke, society is the source of moral sentiments, and his polemic against "abstract reasoning" begins to seem very much like an attack on what classical and Christian traditions have understood as reason itself. In Burke, reason is not a faculty which can ascertain "truth" by which the social order can be brought under judgment. In his view, the organization of government is a matter of convenience and convention. As appalled as Burke would have been by Marx, his assumptions are strikingly similar to Marx's claim that "the human essence is no abstraction in each single individual but the ensemble of social relations."

Burke writes in the *Reflections* : "The moment you abate anything from the full rights of men, each to govern himself, and suffer any artificial, positive limitation upon those rights, from that moment the whole organization of government becomes a consideration of convenience." Alasdair MacIntyre has described the ways in which moral reasoning has today been replaced by "modern emotivism." On this score it may be said that Burke is a modern emotivist, or, more cautiously, that Burke is conventionally invoked in the service of modern emotivism. The use of Burke is "conservative" in that it is a conventionalized emotivism that is marked by a distinct prejudice in favor of the past.

To be fair, there is considerable debate over how to understand Burke. Leo Strauss, for example, viewed Burke as a through-and-through historicist who dismissed transcendent standards of truth in favor of the givens of convention and historical process. Strauss went so far as to claim that Burke prepared the way for Hegel. In *The Morality of Consent*, Alexander Bickel joined many others who interpret Burke's devotion to history and tradition not as historicism or conventionalism but as a way of discerning the manifestations of the good as they appeared in time. Bickel's is perhaps the more charitable view, drawing not unreasonable inferences from what Burke wrote, but I am inclined to think that Strauss has the better of the argument.[2]

But let us not get bogged down in disputes about Burke. Suffice it that, in the view of the world under discussion, reason, not to mention revelation, gives us no purchase, no place to stand, to bring critical judgment to bear on the way things are. What Thomas Aquinas calls the "substitute intelligence" of insects and animals takes over. Reason does not participate in any higher truth, or at least not in any higher truth that is pertinent to the ordering of our life together. John Hallowell, in *The Moral Foundation of Democracy*, has argued persuasively that "the revolt against reason" has been accelerated in this century.[3] Pareto, Marx, Freud, and a legion of epigones in every field of inquiry have persuaded most of our contemporaries that the "good reasons" we give for thinking and doing what we think and do have little connection with the "real reasons." The mandate to debunk, which has dominated modern intellectuality, has led to a situation in which all becomes tautology. All reference to realities outside the self are, in fact, references to the self. We are not really looking at this or that, but are looking at the self looking at the self looking, *ad infinitum*. And so it is that Lewis Carroll wondered whether the bird, flying in ever narrowing circles until it disappears into its own fundament, is tickled by its feathers. Many thinkers today do indeed declare themselves tickled by the feathers of reason disappearing into their arguments against reason.

The radical turn to the human, and ultimately to the self, is sometimes described as the triumph of humanism. Humanism is a term of great nobility. We might say that it is not possible to be more humanistic than the Christian proposition that God became human. There is an argument of venerable vintage that makes the claim that the most radical turn toward humanity is a logical consequence of the Christian doctrine of the incarnation. Since God became incarnate in Jesus Christ, we are no longer to think of a God "up there" or "out there." God has, decisively and without remainder, become human. Precisely on the basis of orthodox doctrine, then, it is claimed that Christian orthodoxy is undone. Because of the incarnation, theology has become anthropology. It follows that secularization, frequently positing itself against Christianity, is in fact the logical consequence of Christianity. Since God is man, man must be God, and then man is indeed the best thing in the world. These nineteenth-century arguments for "secular Christianity" enjoyed a brief revival in the 1960s. While the "death of God theologies" of that era now have a musty odor, their aftermath continues to have a powerful influence in Christian thinking.

In the 1960s revival of this way of thought, frequent reference was made to the "kenotic" tradition in Christian theology. The *kenosis* or self-emptying of God in the man Jesus found its prime biblical expression in the second chapter of Philippians. "Have this mind among yourselves, which you have in Christ Jesus, who though he was in the form of God, did not count equality with God a thing to be grasped, but emptied himself, taking the form of a servant, being born in the likeness of men. And being found in human form he humbled himself and became obedient unto death, even death on a cross." Some who invoked that passage, however, failed to cite what immediately follows. "Therefore God has highly exalted him and bestowed on him the name which is above every name, that at the name of Jesus every knee should bow, in heaven and on earth and under the earth, and every tongue confess that Jesus Christ is Lord, to the glory of God the Father."

The self-emptying of divinity into humanity is not the self-demolition of divinity. Rather, the transcendent becomes immanent so that the immanent might become transcendent. In this connection, more and more Western theologians are coming to appreciate the Eastern Orthodox emphasis on the "divinization" of the human. The *kenosis* of Philippians 2 is only understandable within a trinitarian understanding of God, and it is in that light that we see its agreement with the gospel and letters of John that accent our human participation in the Second Person of the Holy Trinity, the crucified and exalted Jesus. Far from the incarnation meaning that theology has become anthropology, anthropology has now become Christology. In this perspective, it becomes possible to say that humanity— understood as humanity "in Christ"—is the best thing in the world. But note that this perspective is only possible by reference to the One who transcends, while also comprehending, the *humanum* known to us from history and our own experience.

Ways of thinking that abandon the reference that is superior to humanity reduce humanity. When human beings on their own think they are the best thing in the world, they become the most pitiable thing in the world, for they alone of all things in the world are conscious of the threat of meaninglessness. To be sure, those of an existentialist bent take this to be the dignity of humanity, making possible the heroic assertion of meaning in the face of meaninglessness. But clearly this is a case of making a virtue out of desperation. In the classical and biblical traditions, meaning is not of our own contrivance, nor is it our own defiant casting of our meanings into the dark of nothingness. Meaning is bestowed, it is in the created ordering of reality, it is there to be recognized and acted upon.

The modern intellectual course of "critical consciousness," of debunking, of refusing to accept whatever can be reasonably doubted, affects also our thinking about politics. Here too Peter Berger is correct in urging that the course of intellectual courage today is not in debunking received meanings but in "debunking the debunkers." Put differently, the old fable must be turned on its head. This time, when all are agreeing that the emperor has no clothes, the daring young boy points out that he is arrayed in splendid apparel. The most splendid articles of his attire are reason and humanity's intuitions of transcendence, by which government is both morally legitimated and morally challenged. Without reason and transcendent truth, politics is brute power, unexamined convention, and magic for the masses.

We witnessed, in the late 1970s, the emergence of what was called the Religious New Right. That militant host arrived on the public stage waving a long forgotten document that it had dusted off and was offering as proof of its theories about what had gone wrong with America. The document was the Humanist Manifesto of 1933. Our cultural elites were embarrassed by being reminded of a manifesto that four decades earlier represented the advanced thinking of a large segment of our cultural elites. This time around, almost nobody rallied to the defense of the Humanist Manifesto. Maybe it was its unfashionable optimism about reason and human nature. Maybe it was the embarrassment of an earlier period that frankly embraced science and technology as a new religion of progress. "Why bring that up?" murmured our cultured observers, evidently caught off guard by religious zealots intent upon reminding us of alternative zealotries.

The Humanist Manifesto is nonetheless an important point of reference for understanding the religio-cultural gyrations of our historical period. Reading the critics of the religious right, one might have thought that the Humanist Manifesto and "secular humanism" were inventions of the fundamentalists. In fact, the 1933 manifesto was subscribed by a broad representation of the most distinguished and influential thinkers in America, led by John Dewey himself. In their wisdom, the signers understood that the state without religion becomes a monster. They therefore proposed what they candidly called a new religion, "the religion of humanism," which they distinguished from "traditional religions" that had done much good (along with much bad) but were no longer able to cope with "the needs of this age."

The manifesto declared, among other things, that: "Religious humanists regard the universe as self-existing and not created. . . . Religion consists of those actions, purposes, and experiences which are humanly significant. . . . The distinction between the sacred and the secular can no longer be maintained. . . . Humanism will take the path of social and mental hygiene and discourage sentimental and unreal hopes and wishful thinking. . . . A socialized and cooperative economic order must be established to the end that the equitable distribution of the means of life be possible. The goal of humanism is a free and universal society in which people voluntarily and intelligently cooperate for the common good. Humanists demand a shared life in a shared world." Heady stuff, that. No "sentimental and unreal hopes," no "wishful thinking" here.

Their religion, the brightest and best of America's intellectual leadership declared, is a "vital, fearless and frank religion capable of furnishing adequate social goals and personal satisfactions." They recognized that the government and our common life must be guided by religion. It happened, however, that their proposed religion was not the religion of the American people. This posed problems for signers who wanted also to affirm that the direction of society should be *democratically* determined. An aristocratic religion is of limited use in a democratic society. In addition, the manifesto did not argue its case but simply set forth its propositions apodictically, as though they were necessary and self-evident truths. These are things that educated people just *know* to be the case. Admittedly, rational argument is difficult to advance if one believes that "man is a part of nature and that he has emerged as the result of a continuous process." If human beings are entirely explained by nature, it is not easy to explain the phenomenon of human beings explaining nature.

Forty years later, in 1973, Humanist Manifesto II took a more sober tack. Intervening events, the signers said, made the original manifesto "seem far too optimistic." Moreover, the new statement eschewed the term religion and the subscribers styled themselves "democratic secular humanists." Apparently the distinction between the sacred and profane could be maintained after all. The signers "disclaim that they are setting forth a binding credo." Claiming to have learned their lessons from the excessive optimism of the past, they declared, "We stand at the dawn of a new age, ready to move farther into space and perhaps inhabit other planets. Using technology wisely, we can control our environment, conquer poverty, markedly reduce disease, extend our life-span, significantly modify our behavior, alter the course of human evolution and cultural development, unlock vast new powers, and provide humankind with unparalleled opportunity for achieving an abundant and meaningful life."

Because the signers are rational and scientific, they know in advance what further inquiry will reveal: "Nature may indeed be broader and deeper than we now know; any new discoveries, however, will but enlarge our knowledge of the natural." With respect to religion and the state, they declared, "The separation of church and state and the separation of ideology and state are imperatives." Their own affirmations, they would have us believe, are scrupulously non-ideological. The overarching goal is for "each person to become, in ideal as well as practice, a citizen of a world community." After Auschwitz, Dresden, and the Gulag, and after the myriad miniatures of each, the signers dauntlessly conclude, "We believe that humankind has the potential intelligence, good will, and cooperative skill to implement this commitment in the decades ahead." Such effusions may be the only alternative to despair, if indeed humanity is the best thing, the only thing, in the world.

Humanist Manifesto II was followed by "A Secular Humanist Declaration" in 1980. But the signers of these documents were not nearly so distinguished a group as the signers of the 1933 original. Perhaps more reflective people had been more shaken by the great terrors of this century. They were no longer so confident of the dogmas of secularism. The more perceptive among them had come to suspect the irrationality of rationalistic scientism, the absolutism of absolute relativism, the parochialism of deracinated universalism, and the fearful dependencies of the totally autonomous. It is also possible, however, that fewer thinkers rallied to the later manifestos because by then "secular humanism" was less a rallying point than a statement of the conventional wisdom. Why make an issue of what had been secured as orthodoxy in the culturally regnant classes? Intellectuals generally do not find much fun in affirming what they recognize as orthodoxies. Then too, perhaps it was thought to be imprudent, in this kind of society, to proclaim the establishment of a ideology that had not been democratically embraced. In the view of many, the 1973 and 1980 statements likely seemed both redundant and unwise.

If anyone doubts that a humanism along the lines adumbrated in these statements has become cultural orthodoxy, he has only to consult textbooks used in state-supported schools, from the early grades through graduate studies. If religion, or the connection between reason and transcendent truth, are mentioned at all, it is usually in passing and clearly dismissive in intent. "At one time people found answers to the great questions of life in religion, but of course this is no longer possible in our increasingly secular society and world." That is a generic assertion to be found in textbooks dealing with everything from sexual ethics to nuclear war to the beginnings of life on the planet. The proposition that America is or is rapidly becoming a secular society, however, has everything going for it except the evidence.

The reaction of the knowledge class to the moral majoritarian complaints about "secular humanism" evidenced both ineptness and dishonesty. The impression was given that the religious right made it all up, that Jerry Falwell wrote the Humanist Manifesto as a foil rather than John Dewey having promulgated it as a faith. The religious right no doubt got some things very wrong. Secular humanism was not and is not a conspiracy hatched by several hundred godless agents in key places who insinuated it into our educational, legal, political, religious, and corporate establishments in order to undermine "Christian America." Just as surely, secular humanism is not the invention of those who rail against it. The question that should claim the attention of thoughtful people is not whether these ideas were and are promulgated (they were and are), but whether these ideas are true.

To his credit, John Dewey's version of pragmatism was not indifferent to the question of truth. When Dewey died in 1952 at ninety-three years of age, he was widely hailed as a thinker who had had more influence than any other in shaping our public life and habits of mind over the near-century of his lifetime. His pragmatism was keenly attuned to elements of the American spirit, such as tolerance, inclusiveness, and unbounded hope. This is powerfully evident in the conclusion of his 1934 testament, *A Common Faith*:

The ideal ends to which we attach our faith are not shadowy and wavering. They assume concrete form in our understanding of our relations to one another and the values contained in these relations. We who now live are parts of a humanity that extends into the remote past, a humanity that has interacted with nature. The things in civilization we most prize are not of ourselves. They exist by grace of the doings and sufferings of the continuous human community in which we are a link. Ours is the responsibility of conserving, transmitting, rectifying and expanding the heritage of values we have received that those who come after us may receive it more solid and secure, more widely accessible and more generously shared than we have received it. Here are all the elements for a religious faith that shall not be confined to sect, class, or race. Such a faith has always been implicitly the common faith of mankind. It remains to make it explicit and militant.[4]

A Common Faith is a creed not untouched by nobility. There is a faint approximation of something like transcendence in the acknowledgment that the things we most prize "are not of ourselves." And there is perhaps an intimation of salvation by grace in the accent on what we have received from "the doings and sufferings" of others. But, of course, Dewey's transcendence, grace, and faith are exhaustively explained by reference to the immanent, by reference to the human story "in which we are a link." But there is no doubt that Dewey, unlike Richard Rorty and others who clutch his mantle today, thought the elements of his proposed common faith to be *true*.

"What is truth?" Pilate's question is today asked with confused hand wringing and, more commonly, with derision. It is frequently declared to be a non-question. And that, we are told, is the truth. The problem is not simply that we are not agreed on what is true, but that we do not share points of reference by which we might deliberate what is and is not true. Further, we are not agreed that this constitutes a problem. Rorty would persuade us that the problem is that we think it is a problem. We should relax, we should adopt the "ironic mode" in recognizing that we do not have available to us the category of truth by which we can give an account of "the good" to which personal and public life should be ordered.[5] There is much to be said for the claim that Nietzsche's time has come round at last, for he prophetically saw the self-deceiving absurdity of continuing to speak about the good and the true after the death of the transcendent referents which alone make sense of such language.

Perhaps we have reached an impasse. Raw emotivism and Rorty's ironic mode are the end of conversation. Rorty urges that, when we encounter people who insist on talking about truth in public, we should try to "josh them out of it." If that fails, we may simply have to declare them crazy and try to prevent them from doing damage to others. However, the great majority of Americans, at whatever level of reflectiveness, surely assume that the distinction between truth and falsehood is not false. They cannot all be joshed out of that conviction or certified as mad. On the other hand, there are formidable obstacles to restoring the discussion of truth in public. Perhaps a beginning is in the sheer public assertion of the possibility of such a discussion. That creates at least a public discussion of the possibility of discussing public truth, which might be a step toward mending the broken conversation.

Such sheer assertion enlists the support of millions who need no convincing that there is an account of the good to which our lives should be ordered. Most of them need no convincing, however, because they have been spared, perhaps blessedly, the experience of thinking through the reasons for not being convinced. The suggestion that we may require the democratic force of the unphilosophical millions may strike us as being unconscionably vulgar. But this is the social reality that can give public salience to the intellectual labors of such as John Rawls, who, while stifling the metaphysics inherent in his theory, strives to offer a transcendent account of the good (most notably, the great good of justice). Whether or not one believes that that account can be constructed in what he calls "the original position" of ignorance about one's place in life, it has a measure of resonance in the actual position in which most people find themselves. The so-called common man is no doubt puzzled that the discovery of the obvious should require such monumental intellectual energy as Rawls expends, but at the same time he is pleased that even philosophers are not impervious to what comes more easily to those who are not professionally trained to make it difficult.

Most Americans simply do not understand why it is so difficult to give an account of the transcendent good. In their own lives, with varying degrees of intellectual sophistication, they operate with such an account every day. They less than half believe those who tell them that such accounts are purely private and have no correspondence with the public order. In the great majority of cases, the operative accounts of the good are explicitly religious in form. There is an enculturated intuition that such accounts must be "sanitized" for public use—arguments in public should not be "sectarian." Most people who are active in public life develop the requisite sanitation skills with relative ease, but they are convinced that public sanitation does not eviscerate the substance of the transcendent truths by which they live also as public actors.

The sheer popular, even populist, assertion of a religiously grounded account of the good frightens many in our cultural elites. There are others in those elites, however, who eagerly welcome it. They may not be believers themselves, but they have come to the conclusion that only religion can counter the cultural deconstructionism of unbridled critical consciousness. They are not like Nietzsche's pitiable "last man" who goes on thinking that the true, the good, and the beautiful can survive the death of God. But they depend on there being many such last men and last women who will, at whatever cost to their own intellectual integrity, keep the old ideas in circulation.

More than that, they count on their many fellow citizens who have not heard, or have not believed, the news of the death of God. In short, they count on religion to sustain the social viability of an account of the good that is no longer, in their judgment, intellectually viable. People who view religion in terms of its social utility sometimes incline to the opinion that religion is a noble lie. Others among them, however, are not much interested in whether or not it is a lie. The public atheist today is, after all, almost an endangered species. The more common view is that religious claims may be a lie or an interesting possibility. It is further agreed that religion is by no means always ennobling. The point is that religion is socially necessary. Schleiermacher's "cultured despisers of religion" are still very much with us. But there seems to be an increasing number of cultured appreciators of religion's usefulness. Of course these categories are not mutually exclusive, and many people are both. Far from being exclusive, a case might be made that valuing religion chiefly for its social utility assumes disdain for the claims of religion—at least for the claims of biblical religion.

Those who look to religion as a kind of *deus ex machina* that will extricate us from our cultural dilemmas may well be disappointed. Religion in America is in large part a carrier of the cultural diseases for which it is supposed to be the cure. The insinuations of all the usual villains— scientism, vulgar pragmatism, reductionist secularism, the techniques of self-actualization—are far advanced in our religious habits of mind and heart. It is said with justice that in some of our churches religious leaders are hesitant to make any religious statement that does not have redeeming worldly merit, usually in terms of a political or psychological payoff. Nevertheless, however vague, uninformed, and incoherent their thinking about it, most Americans believe that there is a transcendent account of the good to which persons and communities are accountable, and they further believe that that account is borne by biblical religion. (The evidence of the perduring religiousness of Americans is summarized in _Unsecular America_[6]). Considered from the viewpoint of theological orthodoxy or sophistication, American popular religion is not very impressive. But in a society that aspires to be, and to a large extent is, democratic, popular religion is a force that cannot be ignored indefinitely. It is a force that should not be ignored at all.

While popular religion, like the religious studies programs in our universities, has largely capitulated to regnant cultural habits, in large sectors of the society it is also what social scientists call an independent variable. Among Orthodox Jews, conservative Protestants, and more traditional Catholics, it provides an alternative and authoritative reading of reality. Orthodox Jews are relatively few in number, but evangelical and fundamentalist Protestants, combined with Catholics who are more than merely "communal Catholics" (Andrew Greeley) add up to more than a hundred million Americans. This makes an enormous difference in our understanding of this society. The variable of religious commitment correlates more closely than any other variable with social and political attitudes. That is to say, if you know someone is a church-going, Bible-reading Baptist, you will also know, with a very high degree of probability, what he thinks about a host of questions disputed in the public arena. As for Catholics, much is made of the finding that, on an issue such as abortion, there is not much difference of opinion between Catholics and the general population. The same research reveals a very dramatic difference, however, when the distinction is made between nominal Catholics and those actively involved in the life of the church.

Even in those sectors of American religion that are not thought to be theologically or socially conservative, there is a frequently vibrant sense of a biblical tradition that provides a place to stand over against the general culture. In the mainline/oldline Protestant churches there is little readiness to accept a substitute religion along the lines of Dewey's religious humanism. Similarly, the "civil religion" that was much discussed in the 1970s found few takers. With relatively few exceptions, Americans already have a religion, or think they do. Those who are more self-confident about possessing a distinctive account of the good that challenges the culture can, over time, encourage a similar confidence in the religious sectors that are now more culturally assimilated.

In *The Restructuring of American Religion*, Robert Wuthnow ably argues that the churches are increasingly aligned along a liberal-conservative divide, as that divide is defined by social and political attitudes in the general culture. Sociologically considered, the growth dynamics strongly favor those on the conservative side of the divide. At the same time, however, even those religious groups that are most at ease in the Zion of American culture affirm symbols and truth claims of great countercultural force. They, too, remember Sinai, the Cross, and the promise of a Kingdom that obviously is not yet. Past experience instructs us that religious awakenings usually come by surprise. A publicly potent religious awakening would no doubt have inestimable consequences for our culture. But, of course, it may not happen.

There are signs of a resurgence of religion and religiously based moral concern in our public life. More than a decade after it first emerged, what was called the Religious New Right, mainly motored by evangelicals and fundamentalists, is by no means exhausted or even in decline. The scary press stories about fundamentalists taking over America are no longer so prominent, mainly because we have become more or less accustomed to their very considerable presence in our public life. In a like manner, the Roman Catholic presence, especially as articulated by the bishops, has become a fixed feature of our public life. To be sure, this has not been universally accepted. The media railings against the "ayatollahs" of fundamentalism in the 1970s and 1980s have now been redirected against the Catholic bishops. In a style reminiscent of the Know Nothings of the last century, in the last decade of this century prestige newspapers launched campaigns against the Catholic Church as an "unAmerican" institution. Pundits wondered out loud whether the First Amendment's free exercise of religion was really meant for institutions as large and "undemocratic" as the Catholic Church. Such protests, frequently hysterical in tone, come from those who were conditioned by the uncomplicated claim—indeed it was taken to be a truism—that ours is a secular society. Such people are in possession of some of the more influential media pulpits, but they are increasingly recognized as voices from the past.

There are, it must be admitted, troubling, possibly dangerous, aspects of the resurgence of religion in public. Especially among some evangelical and fundamentalist activists, there is a tendency to make a quick and facile move from biblical prescription to public policy. There is even a small but influential group of "Christian Reconstructionists," also called "theonomists," who would replace the constitutional order with an order based on "Bible law." Such groups are a threat, although I believe only a very marginal threat, to the constructive role of religion and religiously informed moral discourse in public life. Their appeal to private, often idiosyncratic, interpretations of "the law of God" is but another form of emotivism.[7]

Religious emotivism is a particularly flammable form of emotivism, calling to mind as it does the wars of religion that virtually destroyed civil society in the sixteenth and seventeenth centuries and prepared the way for the reaction of militantly secularist forms of the Enlightenment. The several biblical traditions, however, have lively resources for the making of genuinely *public* arguments. Those resources are in concepts such as natural law, common grace, general revelation, orders of creation, and the adequacy of human reason for the right ordering of the *polis*. These concepts point to the ways in which believer and nonbeliever, regenerate and unregenerate, can engage one another in a shared world of discourse. Jewish thinkers such as Rabbi David Novak of the University of Virginia have underscored similar conceptual resources in Judaism, with special reference to the common ground established by the "Noahide" commandments.[8]

An interesting twist is that, were these conceptual resources more creatively employed, biblical religion's impact upon our public life would be less ostensibly "religious" than Dewey's religious humanism or Marx's eschatological hope for the Kingdom of Freedom. In other words, arguments from natural law or common grace do not make an appeal to any authority that bears the label "religious." They appeal to reason. In the abortion debate, for example, the Catholic bishops are adamant in saying that they are not making a religious argument for the protection of the unborn.

The question of what is human life is clearly answered by science, and the question of who belongs to the community for which we accept common responsibility could hardly be more clearly a question of public justice. Yet, because it is the bishops saying it, it is deemed to be a "religious" argument that represents "sectarian" teaching derived from revelation. A hundred years ago, at the height of the debate over Darwin and evolution, the great issue was the putative conflict between reason and revelation. Most educated people have had their minds formed by that conflict. Religion is ordered by revelation, they were taught to think, and the public realm is ordered by reason. It is very difficult for them to grasp the fact that now, a hundred years later, it is the institutions of religion that have become the defenders of reason in public discourse.

Where transcendent religion is vibrant, and where such religion defends the integrity of reason, the state is sharply limited in its exercise of magic and mystery. The secular realm, as distinct from the sacred, is both respected and kept within bounds. An effective check is placed upon the sacralizing of politics, and upon the politicizing of the sacred. Admittedly, these distinctions, tensions, and balances are always getting out of whack with one another. Just when we think we have them finely tuned and in proper working order, some new circumstance erupts and we have to go back to square one. We have to rethink again the subtle connections between transcendent and immanent, sacred and secular, private and public, reason and revelation. This rethinking is not done in the expectation that this time we are going to get it right once and for all. We will never get it completely right—or, better, it will never be put completely right—until the promised consummation of history in the Kingdom of God.

Christians have had a number of ways of making these connections over two millennia, and Jews had other ways before that. Until God establishes the absolutely right way, all our ways will be tentative, provisional, and somewhat experimental. The nature of the peculiarly American experiment is exemplified in the First Amendment. The usual formula for the genius of the American arrangement is "the separation of church and state." Regrettably, in recent decades the arrangement has been thrown into disarray by the unprecedented subordination of the "free exercise" provision to the "no establishment" provision of the First Amendment. (Another major problem is posed by *Oregon v. Smith* of 1990, the so-called "peyote case," in which the Supreme Court seemed to eviscerate "free exercise" of its constitutional meaning altogether. That, however, may be a short-term aberration and, in any event, cannot delay us here.)

The result of subordinating free exercise to no establishment—of interpreting the separation of church and state to mean the separation of religion from public life—is to turn religion's constitutional privilege into a constitutional impediment. The result of that, in turn, has been an unnatural constriction of the democratic process by excluding from court and legislature the religiously grounded beliefs of the American people. The state presumes to define the sources from which people may draw the viewpoints that they would advance in the public arena. They may draw their views from Darwin, Marx, Freud, or the comic strip, but, if they are drawn from a source that is identifiably "religious," such views are to be disallowed.

Of course this reasoning is bizarre, but it has insinuated itself into much confused thinking about the separation of church and state. When the ultimacies, including religious ultimacies, to which the people subscribe are excluded from the public order, the state cannot resist the temptation to get into the business of what Cassirer calls mystery and magic. This is not simply because the modern state is ambitious and possessed of the lust for power, although such dynamics should not be underestimated. It is more importantly because someone must articulate in public the meanings by which the society is given a sense of moral legitimacy and purpose.

A somewhat irreverent way of putting the matter is that the state should leave mystery and magic to the institutions of religion, and it should get on with the technical business of governing. But of course governing has never been a purely technical exercise. Today it is technology, among other factors, that forces the state to recognize the impossibility of being "value neutral." Questions of defining life and death and who belongs to the human community are coming at us with disconcerting rapidity. These are on top of older and perduring questions about the moral basis of human rights and state authority. Then there is the continuing, indeed intensifying, set of disputes over the beliefs and moral judgments that should be transmitted in state-controlled education. Herein lies a key component of our dilemma: At the very time when questions of great and irrepressible moral moment are forcing themselves upon us we discover that we do not have shared ideas or even a shared vocabulary for their public deliberation. That is to say, we do not have such shared ideas or vocabulary *if* we exclude from the public square the religiously informed beliefs of the American people. In that case, we perpetuate a political theory and practice that are premised upon an assumption that is devoid of democratic legitimacy, namely, the assumption that human beings are the best thing in the world.

Until the early part of this century there was a "sacred canopy" (Berger) over the American experiment. The experiment had long been guided by what Max Stackhouse has described as the Lockean-Puritan synthesis.[9] That synthesis brought together contractual private interest and covenantal public purpose. In addition, the synthesis was joined to a commonsense philosophy of Enlightenment reason that was hospitable to biblical religion, and in fact understood itself to be the natural adjunct of Christianity.[10] To be sure, the result may have been something of an intellectual mishmash at times, and nobody would mistake the resulting public deliberation for the intellectually stately discourse that Aristotle or Plato thought appropriate to the *polis*. American democracy, perhaps any democracy, is in some respects a rough and raucous enterprise.

In the great testing of the nineteenth century, the dispute over slavery, civil discourse gave way to civil war. Under pressures of no less moment than slavery, it is not entirely alarmist to think that could happen again. There is certainly very little publicly articulate moral consensus in America today. An argument is made that in our day-by-day practice, in the functioning of our institutions, and in our operating assumptions there is in fact more of a moral consensus at work than might be indicated by our apparent inability to articulate what that consensus is. The argument has merit, but it does seem to offer only the slight consolation that we might be able to muddle through for a while longer. A consensus that cannot be articulated cannot be renewed, and it cannot be transmitted

to the successor generation. Those who believe that we
have irretrievably lost the consensus that we once had
tend to respond in one of three ways. First, some advance
the incredible proposal that a society can get along without shared points of reference for moral deliberation in
public. Second, some propose the establishment of what
amounts to a new public religion—whether called secular
humanism, religious humanism, or civil religion. The third
response is to say that the jig is up with this experiment
in liberal democracy.

There is a more promising response. Part of it requires
a fundamental rethinking of the role of religion in our
public life in order to restore a more natural interaction
between public discourse and popular belief. Another part
of the response requires committed Jews and Christians to
rethink the ways in which a biblical worldview can be
translated into public language about the right ordering
of the *polis*. The great need is to create, or recreate, a
religiously informed public philosophy for the American
experiment in ordered liberty. Walter Lippmann's somewhat similar call in 1955 was entirely to the point,[11] as we
can also affirm aspects of John Dewey's intuition in calling
for "a common faith."

Lippmann recognized the importance of "natural law"
in public discourse, but for many reasons—not least his
painful ambivalence about his Jewishness—could not bring
himself to make the connections between natural law language and its basis of democratic legitimation in religion.
Dewey, on the other hand, had a strong appreciation of
the religion factor. Since he did not share the "traditional"
beliefs of most Americans, however, he rather improba-
bly proposed himself as the founder of a new religion.
That proposal found few takers outside the relatively small
world of those who, like Dewey, longed to maintain the
cohesive force of the Protestant pulpit without the bother
of Christian doctrine.

Alongside the religion factor, the public philosophy that we need calls for the renewal of philosophy itself. Given the state of academic philosophy, this is admittedly somewhat hard to envision. Professional philosophers have, for the most part, locked themselves into the iron cage of analytical reductionism, while others, still getting paid as philosophers, say that philosophy has been replaced by literary criticism in the deconstructionist mode. Perhaps it is vain to hope that academic philosophy will reconnect itself with the history of philosophy, taking up again the classical questions of what we can know, what we can hope for, and what we ought to do. It is worth remembering, however, that the announcement of the death of philosophy is a perennial and should be received with a measure of skepticism. Even the most reduced of analytical philosophies, for instance, contain seeds that can grow and press against the stifling constrictions of regnant theological orthodoxies.

Alasdair MacIntyre writes,

> What makes all the different types of analytic philosophy *analytic* is their common preoccupation with meanings; what makes them all *philosophy* is . . . the historical continuity of the way these preoccupations are embodied. Cause, personal identity, the nature of belief, and what goodness is are topics that continually recur in the context of discussions about speech-acts, logical form, and extensionality. If we say that David Lewis is a remarkable philosopher, what makes him remarkable may be his own, but what makes him a philosopher is precisely the relationship of his work to that of Leibniz.[12]

And, MacIntyre would likely not object to our adding, the relationship of his work to that of Jonathan Edwards, Calvin, Aquinas, Augustine, and Aristotle.

MacIntyre's confidence about the persistent recurrence of the classical questions is shared by only a minority of contemporary philosophers. Richard Weaver famously said that ideas have consequences. If ideas were the only thing that had consequences, and if the history of ideas were entirely contained within itself, it would seem that the chances are slight that this minority of philosophers will make much difference. In that case it would make sense, as MacIntyre has sometimes suggested, to abandon the public square to the barbarians who are now in possession of it, and to seek out small communities where we can live the life of virtue and reason while waiting for the arrival of "a new Saint Benedict."

Fortunately, other forces, including the religious and social forces we have been discussing, also have consequences. In addition, if the great questions of philosophy are neglected by professional philosophers, they will be taken up by others. They are being taken up in a very impressive manner by theologians such as Wolfhart Pannenberg, for whom theology is the "science of meaning" in intense conversation with the history of philosophy. Human beings are incorrigibly inquirers about meaning. Human beings are also incorrigibly social, forming arrangements for life together. A society cannot long survive if it cannot give a persuasive account of itself in terms of meaning that transcends itself.

Asked to give such an account of the ordering of our life together, most contemporary thinkers become tongue-tied and stammering, and then take refuge in erudite disputes about the meanings of meaning. This state of affairs cannot last for long, or else this way of ordering our life together will not last for long. The Puritans, the Founders, Lincoln, and our foremost intellectuals were all confident that they could give such an account of the American experiment. The ability to give such an account was, with exceptions, confidently assumed until about the middle of the twentieth century. The notion that such an account is unnecessary or impossible is relatively recent.

Most of us, I expect, have not in a deliberative manner arrived at the conclusion that such an account is unnecessary or impossible. Rather, in a fit of absentmindedness, we simply forgot that such an account is necessary and possible. As Dr. Johnson reminds us, humankind has a greater need to be reminded than to be instructed. We need to be reminded today that giving an account of liberal democracy—its ethos, laws, and politics—begins by reference to a higher good. And that reference, Aristotle reminds us, presupposes reason's perception that we are not the best thing in the world.

3. Remembering
the Movement

Generations come and go with great rapidity. As noted, we are told that student generations last four years, at the most. In 1970 I was speaking at a prestigious liberal arts college in the Midwest and mentioned in passing the high hopes for racial justice created by Selma. From the looks of incomprehension, it was obvious that most of the audience had not the slightest idea of what I was talking about. For those of us involved in them, events such as the great civil rights march in Selma, Alabama, barely five years earlier, were etched in our minds, and we thought in the minds of all, as benchmarks of historical change. Suddenly this writer, then in his early thirties, felt very old.

When I was a boy, I loved to hear my parents talk about "the olden days." The olden days were the early 1930s, the years immediately prior to my birth. For today's college student the 1960s are very much the olden days. Talking about them serves more than the purposes of nostalgia. The 1930s were the heyday of what was once called the Old Left. Up until the 1960s, the alliances and hostilities of the 1930s pretty much defined the intellectual disputes between Stalinists and anti-Stalinists, Trotskyites and anti-Trotskyites. I almost said between socialists and capitalists but, until the 1970s, a serious intellectual defender of capitalism was hard to find. When one reads a memoir such as Sidney Hook's magnificent *Out of Step,* one is taken back to those earlier decades, to the olden days, to times of definitional force that still exert an influence over our own time.

The 1960s were like that, although with much greater impact on the religious communities in America. The world of what Irving Howe called "The New York Intellectuals," with all its Old Left disputes, was in large part a Jewish affair. The New Left was a much more ecumenical affair, so to speak. More than two decades later, that New Left is now our Old Left, and it still exerts a powerful influence, just as the first Old Left continued to be a major force thirty years after it peaked. The New Left of the 1960s was very much a Jewish-Protestant affair, with the Protestant factor in the ascendancy because of the connection with the black church. The New Left, it should be remembered, both converged with, and was precipitated by, the civil rights movement. Many, with some justice, remember that crusade as the last great movement for social change in America that was morally unambiguous.

Roman Catholics played an increasingly important part in what came to be called "The Movement" in the 1960s. The formidable Dorothy Day with her Catholic Worker movement was, it seemed, an omnipresent icon. It was hard to find a Catholic activist who had not been started, in one way or another, by Dorothy Day. In the mid-1960s I spoke at one of her Friday evening gatherings at the Catholic Worker on the Lower East Side of Manhattan. Ecumenism was not taken for granted in those days, and having a Lutheran pastor as speaker was considered worthy of comment. In her introduction, Dorothy Day remarked that she admired Martin Luther as a rebel, and it was only unfortunate that he got into questions of religion. Unlike many Catholic activists of the time, Dorothy Day was emphatically Catholic, rigorously orthodox in theology and traditional in piety.

Father Daniel Berrigan was a good friend then. He and I, together with Rabbi Abraham Joshua Heschel, became the first chairmen of Clergy Concerned About Vietnam in the fall of 1964. (Much later to become Clergy and Laity Concerned, an organization of a dramatically different ideological coloration.) Dan and his brother Philip, also a priest at the time, were to become perhaps the most celebrated Catholic figures in The Movement. Both were to spend prolonged periods in jail for pouring blood on draft cards and military equipment, among other things. Being arrested and doing at least a little time in jail was *de rigueur* for activists of the period. When I spoke around the country, the introduction routinely included a reference to my having been arrested and jailed in half a dozen cities. It was a kind of credential. I was always uneasy about that, since being arrested seemed an easy enough thing to do, and one wanted to be taken seriously for what one had to say, not for having demonstrated one's "commitment." Commitment was a very big word then. It still is, I suppose.

What is now called Evangelicaldom was not a significant factor in The Movement. Events such as the Chicago declaration on evangelical social responsibility were to await the early 1970s. A self-confessed evangelical, never mind fundamentalist, in the civil rights or anti-war campaigns was a find. One day I introduced Jim Wallis, then launching the Sojourners movement, to the late Eugene Carson Blake. Gene Blake had for many years been Mr. Liberal Protestant, having led both the National Council of Churches and the World Council of Churches for years. Probably more than anybody of the time, he embodied the liberal Protestant mainline that was, with astonishing rapidity, later to become the oldline and then the sideline of American religion. Blake was greatly intrigued that Wallis was an evangelical who also called himself a radical. He found the combination entirely improbable. "Give it a little time," he told Wallis, "and you'll come over to our side." I could have kicked him, but I didn't. Later I tried to explain to Blake that we should not want evangelicals to become liberal Protestants but, rather, to bring the hosts of evangelicaldom into the movement for social change. Gene Blake thought that a completely improbable prospect, and maybe he was right.

This is one person's reflection on The Movement, and it is unabashedly subjective. But perhaps it will be of more than purely personal interest. There is a direct line between The Movement and the lines of agreement and disagreement in the churches today on questions of Christian social responsibility. Many of the major actors then are major actors now. Most of the people I went to jail with then are still around, usually as tenured professors in academe or running oldline church offices in what the late Paul Ramsey called "the church-and-society curia." Then, as now, people were much preoccupied by "positioning" themselves in relation to the ideological labels and arguments of the day. In the early 1960s, I declared that I hoped always to be religiously orthodox, culturally conservative, politically liberal, and economically pragmatic. That "quadrilateral" still seems to make a good deal of sense. The main change over the years has been in what people mean by politically liberal.

For me, The Movement really began in 1961 when, at age twenty-five, I became pastor of St. John the Evangelist, a black parish straddling the Williamsburg and Bedford-Stuyvesant sections of Brooklyn. We sometimes called it St. John the Mundane, in order to distinguish it from St. John the Divine, the Episcopal cathedral up on Morningside Heights. Those years in black Brooklyn still seem, and maybe will always seem, like the glory years. And a large part of the glory was immersion in the movement of black aspiration that had been launched in the South a few years earlier under the leadership of Dr. Martin Luther King, Jr. Later, in the two years prior to his death in 1968, I would work closely with Dr. King as he was striving to bring the Southern movement to the North, and to merge it with the powerful dynamics of the movement against the war in Vietnam. That is a long and fascinating tale, and someday, if I reach whatever age is seemly to be writing memoirs, I hope to give an account of it.

The immediate point is that, for me, The Movement of the 1960s was about two things: racial justice and world peace. That is not the way many other people remember The Movement. One comedian currently gets a big laugh when he observes, "If you remember the sixties, you weren't there." He is referring to a very different side of The Movement, The Movement of drugs, rock, sex, and drugs. That side of The Movement was rich in slogans. "Don't trust anyone over thirty," for example. (A slogan that, for obvious reasons, had a short-lived attraction for those who promulgated it.) "Make Love Not War" seemed to be ubiquitous. Another was, "Let it all hang out." My friend Peter Berger, the sociologist, said at the time that his motto was, "Tuck it all back in," and I had some sympathy for that. (Remember the "cultural conservatism" in the above-mentioned quadrilateral.)

For me, The Movement was personified in Dr. King. You can get a good argument on the subject from people who knew him, some of them much better than I, but I did not see much conflict between Dr. King and my quadrilateral. By some standards, it may seem preposterous to suggest that Dr. King was "religiously orthodox." But Taylor Branch,[1] among others, has made the point that, within the context of his theological training, he was remarkably orthodox. In view of his now much publicized sexual dalliances, his "cultural conservatism" might seem equally implausible. But it seems clear to me that Dr. King knew such activity reflected his weakness; he knew he was a sinner. It would have been alien and repugnant to him to suggest that he was a proponent of "alternative life-styles," as they came to be called, with respect to sexuality and family life. He was no radical when it came to the bourgeois norms of his black Baptist childhood. I recall his thinking it delightfully daring when, in a restaurant, he would smoke a cigarette or two.

"Politically liberal"—that he certainly was, even if in a time when most liberals had been "radicalized," as the jargon of the day had it. As for "economically pragmatic," there is considerable dispute about that. Some writers claim that, at the time of his death, he was moving and moving rapidly toward a more "radical analysis" of a distinctly socialist and Marxist nature. I remain skeptical. From his writings and from personal conversations, I believe Dr. King had no serious complaint about democratic capitalism, if only it could be more democratic by including the poor in its opportunities. The Poor Peoples Campaign of 1968, which he did not live to lead, was aimed at achieving "rights in life" as well as "rights in law." Although there were many associated with that effort who made no secret of their desire for a radical and socialist restructuring of "the system," my impression is that Dr. King understood himself to be testing and pressing, not repudiating, the American political and economic order.

Admittedly, that is a very affirmative depiction of Dr. King. I have no doubt that I tended to see in him what I wanted to see. But the reader will understand if I feel no obligation to go into the subject "warts and all." This is not a biography of Dr. King but one person's reflection on The Movement that he thought to be personified in Dr. King. As I look back on it now, for me The Movement ended, or at least it was clearly ending, in 1968. It was not only the death of Dr. King. That summer I was a delegate to the Democratic National Convention in Chicago. While I was pledged to Eugene McCarthy, I was hoping to support Robert Kennedy, but he too had been killed earlier that summer. At the convention, and against the rules imposed by Mayor Richard Daley, I joined in leading a large group of delegates in a protest march down Michigan Avenue. We all ended up in Cook County jail cells, where we listened on radio to Hubert Humphrey's acceptance speech in which he invoked the Prayer of St. Francis of Assisi. "Make me an instrument of Thy peace," he intoned, but the mood in the jail cells was more angry than prayerful.

In the 1970s we began to hear a lot about "single issue politics," mainly in connection with the protest against abortion. It is sometimes forgotten how unremitting was the "single issue politics" of The Movement in 1968. The single issue, of course, was Vietnam. Within The Movement few dissented from the proposal that, no matter how much he had later turned against the war, Humphrey had to be penalized for supporting the war during his years as vice president under Lyndon Johnson, even if it meant the election of Richard Nixon. I am sorry to say that I was not among the dissenters on that. But I was, with difficulty, becoming accustomed to my role as a dissenter on much else respecting The Movement.

To the extent that I was kept honest about the anti-war protest, it was largely due to the aforementioned Paul Ramsey of Princeton. He insisted that he was not arguing in favor of U.S. policy, but he was equally insistent that the protest against that policy was not self-evidently valid. In numerous arguments going on late into the night, he convinced me that we in The Movement were neither so right nor so righteous as we sometimes thought. He also helped me and many others to understand the critical difference between morality and moralism, especially in relation to questions of war and peace.

Morality requires discipline, discernment, and the offering of good reasons. Moralism is the indulgence of sentimental and often egotistic judgments that are tantamount to little more than what we have been calling emotivism. One of the unhappy legacies of the Vietnam years is the license it gave to public moralisms. Every conflict was pronounced to be a great "moral issue." Today, issues are defined as "moral issues" not by moral reasoning but simply by turning up the volume on the public effusion of our feelings. A moral issue, in short, is what you *really* feel strongly about.

But back to The Movement. In the 1968 "War of Chicago," public attention was focused on the armies of the counterculture, as it was called. It became apparent in Chicago that the primary public perception, or at least the media perception, of The Movement no longer had to do with racial justice and the establishment of a more peaceful world order. The focus had shifted to the "student revolution" whose leaders defined The Movement in terms of liberation from their own oppression by "the System." For many of them, the liberating alternative was represented by North Vietnam and its leader, Ho Chi Minh. After we returned to the convention, late one night in a hotel room over a cold Heineken, Murray Kempton, a New York columnist, and I pondered our awkwardness in having to spend as much time, it seemed, in distancing ourselves from others in The Movement as in distancing ourselves from the opponents of The Movement. That conversation still stands out, maybe because it was the first time the question was framed in quite that way.

In 1979 Norman Podhoretz would publish *Breaking Ranks,*[2] which is an account of his sometimes painful discovery that he was no longer "a man of the Left." By 1979 ranks had been breaking for some time. My first serious encounter with that experience came in 1967 when I published in *Commonweal,* the liberal Catholic magazine, "Abortion: The Dangerous Assumptions." This, my brothers and sisters in The Movement quickly made clear in no uncertain terms, was heresy. At that time, the move toward "liberalized abortion," as it was called, was on the ascendancy, and there was to be no doubt that it was one of "our" issues. I knew it was not one of my issues. From that time on, it was made evident to me in ways both subtle and direct that I was thought by some to be something of a security risk in The Movement. I continued to hold office in myriad organizations. (Among the most lasting impressions of The Movement is the thousands of hours spent in meetings—meetings prolonged by The Movement's penchant for "participatory democracy," which means they usually lasted until everyone was too exhausted to go on any more.) But offices and writings and innumerable public speeches notwithstanding, I was increasingly aware that I had left The Movement or, what seemed more likely, that The Movement had left me.

At one of the great "Mobilizations for Peace" in Washington, I was sitting on the platform next to Norman Thomas. It was only months before the death of this extraordinary man who had repeatedly run for president on the socialist ticket and had inspired many of the Left, both Old and New. At age eighty-five, he thought he had seen almost everything, but he was clearly shaken by the spectacle of protestors burning the American flag. "Don't they understand," he asked with tears brimming, "that our purpose is to cleanse the flag, not to burn it?" The answer is that some of them did understand that that was his purpose. It was not theirs.

In truth, there had always been deep disagreements, indeed fissures, in The Movement. As long as it was believable that the focus on racial justice and world order could be maintained, it seemed expedient to ignore or downplay those differences. By the end of the sixties I had pretty well concluded that that focus had been lost and could not be restored. In 1975 I would muster whatever support I still had in what was still left of The Movement to join with James Forest of the Fellowship of Reconciliation in issuing a public protest against Hanoi's brutal repression of the Vietnamese people following the U.S. withdrawal. We asked 104 nationally prominent anti-war protestors to join us. The response indicated a division of almost exactly 50–50. Such a protest was heresy in the view of those who subscribed to the maxim, "No criticism to the Left." But in those circles I had by then little credibility to lose. Several years earlier in *The Christian Century*, for which I then wrote regularly, I had published "The Loneliness of the Long Distance Radical," a bittersweet retrospective on what had been The Movement.[3]

"Precisely when 'the movement' ended is a matter of lively conjecture," I wrote then. "Some cite the death of Martin King, others the '68 Democratic Convention, yet others the orgiastic murders at Altamont [a drug and rock concert] as the moment of truth. But whatever the month and year, *that* the movement, as we conceived of it in the second half of the '60s, is dead is a fact; and recognition of the fact is a necessary premise to understanding the 'new politics' of the '70s." And, because the postures, labels, presuppositions, and alignments perdure into the present, understanding what happened to The Movement is necessary to understanding our situation also today.

Three years before my farewell-to-all-that in the *Century*, in 1968 to be precise, I had written with Peter Berger *Movement and Revolution.*[4] Berger's part of the book was written from the viewpoint of a political skeptic (the term "neoconservative" having not yet been invented) and mine from the viewpoint of a "radical." I then defined The Movement as "the cluster of persons, organizations, worldviews and activities located on what is conventionally called the Left and acting in radical judgment upon the prevailing patterns, political, economic, social, and moral, of American life." At the time I was rather pleased with that definition, and some may find it satisfactory still. But I am now convinced that it was too generalized, assuming more than I made explicit.

I assumed greater political and moral cohesiveness on the part of The Movement's adherents than subsequent events bore out. Already by 1968 it was evident that The Movement was mainly a mood in search of social reality. The mood was clearly "revolutionary." Whether in student takeovers of administration buildings, or in the bombing of research laboratories, or in the rage of young blacks burning down their neighborhoods, "revolution" was in the air. In *Movement and Revolution,* I applied the classical criteria of a "justified war" to a "justified revolution." It was intended as a cautionary counsel, warning against facile and faddish calls for revolution. In revolutions, after all, people do get killed, and activists who claim to be a "peace movement" should think twice, at least twice, about being party to killing people.

Those times were not friendly to cautionary counsels, however. Not that the book was not well received. It was. But, to my regret, many reviewers and readers tended to miss the cautionary counsel and took it as a theoretical legitimation of revolution. To my regret, I say, because I see now that the caution should have been much more emphatic. The sorry fact is that in 1968, when the book was written, I still thought it necessary to protect my standing in The Movement, and I did that by employing a radical tone that, for many readers, obscured the cautionary substance. The fault was mine, and the fault flowed from an anxiety. The anxiety was that people might think that I had "sold out." The accusation of "selling out" was very intimidating then, as it is now. In a time when one's associates were earnestly claiming to be more-radical-than-thou, one felt the need to give assurances that one was at least as radical as he was before. But of course I was not. More accurately, I was being led to a quite different understanding of what it means to be radical.

The Movement was pervasively self-congratulatory, much given to celebrating itself as a historically unique actualization of the good, the true, and the beautiful. It was a substitute church for thousands of people; good people, for the most part, who were in poignant search of a community that could bear their hopes and fears and sense of being. For some of us that was from the beginning a source of tension in our relationship to The Movement. Our difficulty with The Movement was that we already had a church. In terms of gathering up all the enthusiasms and passions of the time, however, the churches did not appear to many to be nearly so comprehensive or compelling as The Movement. In fact, the religiously oriented sectors of The Movement portrayed themselves as communities of truly catholic reach. Elsewhere, catalogues of Movement offerings abounded, an outstanding example being Mitchell Goodman's *The Movement Toward A New America: The Beginnings of a Long Revolution.*[5]

The pages of that large book are brittle and yellowed now, and we must make an effort to remember how fresh and promising it seemed to many then. But these celebratory catalogues also, albeit inadvertently, exposed the bankruptcy of the radical corporation in which so many had invested their lives, fortunes, and sacred honor. Well, at least a part of their lives. And they had then no fortunes to lose. And "honor" was not a word that appeared in the lexicon of The Movement. Displayed in such catalogues was a collection of radicalia, revealing not simply a lack of order or rationality in The Movement, but the existence of numerous "revolutions," most of which, were they to succeed, would cancel out others that had equal claim to representing The Movement. The Movement had become a zero sum game.

It was proclaimed, frequently at the same time and by the same people, as a movement toward unbridled individualism and centrally directed social discipline; toward revolutionary asceticism and the celebration of polymorphous perversity; toward minority separatism and determined universalism. Its symbols were, alternately and often simultaneously, the clenched fist, the clasped hands of different color, the two-finger peace sign, the one-finger "one way" sign, the rifle (with or without the flower in the barrel), a clenched fist inside the circle of the female logogram, and a vasectomized (i.e., ecologically innocent) *penis erectus*. All of these were offered as signs of "organized rage against systemic oppression" and were flaunted to the accompaniment of insistent demands for "radical commitment" to "liberation."

I confess to being a little embarrassed to mention another book in the telling of this story, but books are a way of continuing the conversation, and marking new stages in the conversation. A book important to some of us was *The*

Geography of Faith, a 1970 conversation between Harvard psychiatrist Robert Coles and Daniel Berrigan.[6] It is really an argument between the two, although a muted one. For Berrigan, the fires of The Movement still burned brightly in the night of "Amerika" and the horror that this country presumably cast over the world. Coles seemed to sense that The Movement was dying. He was suspicious of the posturings of its leaders, he was candid about the "beautiful people" who rode off into the sunset toward wilderness communes, he was unillusioned about "prophets" and "revolutionaries" in search of university tenure, he was bemused by radical graduate students writing dissertations on why the "free universities" failed and how it should be done differently "the next time." Coles contrasted all that with the people he had come to know who represented a different kind of movement. He pointed to those who were quietly, relentlessly, working in southern countrysides and northern ethnic communities to build economic cooperatives, health services, and the sinews of community responsibility in education and other fields. Then and now, Robert Coles has a rare talent for attending to the particular, of catching, through the noise of grand propositions, the voices of people.

A different kind of radicalism was emerging, a radicalism that did not need to be propped up by The Movement, a minority radicalism. These different radicals were critically distanced from the tribal consciousness fostered by a Movement that offered to embrace all comers and turn them into instant brothers and sisters. The community of the redeemed that once seemed so inexorable and consoling had been dissipated. These different radicals knew that in The Movement they had no abiding city. It seemed possible that a new kind of leadership was emerging, composed of people who knew what The Movement forgot, that radicalism is always a minority vocation. It is not the personal search for community or self-fulfillment, but the surrender of self for particular others—in which surrender one finds a self and a community that abide. The devotion of such radicals is not shaped, nor even buoyed or deflated for long, by the numbers. The people who can be counted on know the loneliness of the long distance radical and have overcome their fear of it. In that overcoming, they discover the enduring community possessed by those who know themselves to be "surrounded by so great a cloud of witnesses" (Hebrews 12).

As The Movement was waning in the early 1970s, there were many of its adherents who openly longed for some new horror that would revive the fevered pitch of rage. Richard Nixon's policy of "Vietnamization," of letting the South Vietnamese bear the brunt of the war, had its intended effect on The Movement. Among the less edifying dynamics of The Movement was the personal fear of the military draft. Only the most naive or mendacious denied that, for hundreds of thousands of draft-deferred students in the peace movement, the goal of peace was vague and misty, whereas the goal of personally staying out of the war was precise and immediate.

At St. John's in Brooklyn in 1966 we held the nation's first service of its kind, in which hundreds of draft cards were turned in, placed on the altar, and then sent to the Pentagon. It received a great deal of national coverage, many of the media incorrectly reporting that draft cards were burned. What was burning in and around the church was marijuana, its sweetish odor mixing with the incense that was at St. John the Mundane among the intimations of the transcendent. The Movement and its media cheerleaders deemed the event a great success. I was not so sure.

On that day, as on most days back then, I thought of my two brothers who were fighting in Vietnam. They and I had earnestly argued about the need for respecting conscientious decisions about the rights and wrongs of the war. I was not sure that the draft card turn-in was as morally earnest as the questions about this war, and all war, deserved. I was not sure that the appropriate distinctions were being made. Rabbi Abraham Joshua Heschel spoke that day. Heschel said then, as he had often said before, "Some are guilty; all are responsible." That day, however, like The Movement of which it was part, was choreographed as a festival of the innocent who proved their innocence by declaring their non-responsibility. It was yet another occasion for pondering the difference between morality and moralism.

Picking through "the rag and bone shop of the heart" (Yeats), earnestness and integrity are hard enough to discern in ourselves, never mind discerning it in others. There were those in The Movement who seemed to be indifferent to the moral quality of protest, so long as the protest itself was maintained. I know that, in saying this, I risk offending some readers now in their forties, fifties, and sixties for whom The Movement was the singular moment of moral luminosity in their lives. But that is the way it was, or so it seems to me.

In the "Long Distance Radical" article, I was critical of Movement colleagues who expressed the wish for some new outrage that would revive the fortunes of the cause. "Some egregiously stupid and brutal action on the part of the government might revive the movement as we remember it," I wrote, "but this is not something to be desired." There were those who said we needed another Cambodia or a dozen more bloody prison riots such as that at the Attica state prison in New York. (In 1972, it seems odd to remember, "Cambodia" referred to Nixon's military "incursion," not to the later genocide perpetrated by Pol Pot and his revolutionary liberators.) I was then not much alarmed by Nixon's political adroitness in taking the edge off The Movement. I wrote that "healthy people cannot live forever in a state of unrelieved indignation and therefore will accept even slight change as improvement enough to justify relaxing for a time."

The counterview is that to relax, to be grateful for one's little place in the grand scheme of things, to notice that the ordinary is touched by the wingtips of angels, is to sell out. The driving fear of The Movement was the fear of being ordinary. "The most abiding determination of my life is that I will not be ordinary," he declared with a force of conviction that I had not noticed in him before. He was the scion of a huge California fortune and one of the many funders of radical causes whom Tom Wolfe would brilliantly satirize in his analysis of "radical chic."

The Black Panthers were among his favorite causes, and he boasted that Huey Newton and others held strategy sessions on his yacht. In his palatial home on a boulevard of palatial homes he explained to me with a wry smile, "Come the revolution, those other places will be people's palaces. I intend to live in mine." He also befriended artists and in his home were works by, among many others, Jasper Johns, Robert Rauschenberg, and David Hockney. He was publicly coy about whether he had been a member of the party, meaning of course the Communist Party USA. But he assured me in leisurely conversation late one night that "the struggle" was the meaning of his life and, whatever happened to The Movement, it was part of a larger movement that could not be stopped. As I am writing this, news came that yesterday he jumped to his death from the twelfth story of a building in Santa Monica. I am told that he was depressed by ill health. I expect his depression had sources deeper than that.

1989 was the year that Abbie Hoffman, the premier clown of what Harvey Cox described as the dionysiac feast of fools that was the 1960s, died of a drug overdose. It was also the twentieth anniversary of the Woodstock Festival, which had been held a few hours north of New York City. On the anniversary, a rash of books and articles appeared looking back on the Woodstock Nation, as it was called. Most of these were celebrative, but at least one book noted with sour nostalgia that several years after the event, on really hot summer days, the pungent smell of human excrement deposited by hundreds of thousands of revellers still wafted over the farm fields neighboring the site where the rock-sated children of the Age of Aquarius believed that history had been changed for once and forever. But for many others the nostalgia was sweet, recalling the moment when they were part of a vast herd of independent minds deliriously certain that they were not, and would never be, ordinary.

We should not be contemptuous of our own youth, for it is the only youth we are going to have. But I believe the survivors of the Woodstock Nation who now have become or are on their way to becoming the senior faculty in our universities and the leaders of our major institutions, including the churches, are quite wrong to point today's youth to the 1960s as a period of exemplary commitment and authenticity. From a moral perspective, it was, for the most part, a slum of a decade. For the most part. The great exception was the civil rights movement as defined by Dr. King. That began in Montgomery, Alabama, in 1956. In the form defined by Dr. King, it was already coming apart in 1965 with the emergence of the black power movement. The passion for reconciliation on the basis of justice was giving way to the frisson of revolutionary rage and the demand for reparations to be exacted by the force of fear. More than two decades later black America, or at least poor blacks in our northern cities, are more radically isolated than ever. The great majority of white Americans finally came to embrace the "dream" articulated by Dr. King at the great March on Washington of August 28, 1963, only to be confronted by a black leadership that, while claiming the mantle of Dr. King, declared that the time for that dream had passed. But more on that later.

There were other putative achievements of the 1960s that made it, we are told, an exemplary period by comparison with which the present is a retreat into apathy, greed, and general banality. There was the ending of the war in Vietnam, the new wave of feminism, the sexual revolution, and the discovery of alternative lifestyles. After the millions of boat people and the genocide on the killing fields of Cambodia, only the most obtuse and desperate

apologists for The Movement will deny that the memory
of the war has assumed a deep moral ambiguity that was
not generally recognized at the time. As for the gender,
sexual, and lifestyle revolutions, enthusiasms must at least
be tempered by our awareness of the millions upon millions of abortions that followed, by the dramatic increase
in fatherless children, especially among the poor, by the
transformation of marriage into serial polygamy, by AIDS,
and by the scourge of drugs. Can all these disasters be
blamed on the 1960s? No. Might they have overtaken us
without the 1960s? Possibly. Those with eyes to see, however, will recognize the connections between the agitated
illogics of that time and the now manifest curses that were
sold to a generation as blessings of the New Freedom.

Religiously orthodox, culturally conservative, politically
liberal, and economically pragmatic. That quadrilateral
made sense then, and makes sense now. Admittedly, it has
become harder to explain since "politically liberal" parted
company from the other three components. The symbolic
times of leave-taking can be specified. One such time was
the third day of the National Democratic Convention of
1972, early in the morning. We delegates to the Miami
convention were among the Americans still awake in the
wee hours when George McGovern made his acceptance
speech. "Come home, America!" was his refrain. I was
seated beside a labor leader, one of those people for whom
"liberal" meant Hubert Humphrey and Henry "Scoop" Jack-
son, and religion and family and patriotism and increased
economic opportunity. Halfway into McGovern's speech,
the union leader leaned over and said, "America *is* at home.
Where are *we* going?" At the time I thought him clever; I
would later come to realize that he was wise.

Here too, America had turned against itself. McGovern
was and is a fundamentally decent person, a Sunday School
teacher and erstwhile Methodist minister. Like so many
in the American progressivist tradition, he was only one
step from the Protestant pulpit. He was a practitioner of

the politics of moralism, and, in reaction to that, more "realistic" politicians would come to refer dismissively to that kind of politics as "the vision thing." Not for McGovern the vicious polemics against "Amerika." And yet, by positing another America to which we were all to come home, he played upon the support of those who declared the real, existent America to be hopelessly corrupted by capitalist rot and imperialist ambition. He knew what he was doing. By positioning himself next to the radicalized, sneering, contemptuous, hordes of the youthful "revolution," he showed himself to be an adult who could come to terms with the future, and the contrast with their vulgar angers displayed to advantage his fundamental decency. At least that seemed to be the strategy of a campaign shaped by the quest for political gain from America's turning against itself.

In the early 1970s, liberal politics institutionalized the ill-joined radicalisms of The Movement after it was evident that The Movement had come apart. The Movement had been tenuously held together by shared moral outrages combined with diverse and often contradictory, but always radical, "analyses of the systemic evils of the system." Yet, mainly, its fragile unity was sustained by slogans of impassioned fatuity, and by the slogans of impassioned fatuity that opposed it. The radical "Make Love Not War" and the conservative "Love It or Leave It" were mutually reinforcing. They would in time be institutionalized in the more strident wings of the two parties, and thus would politics debase a cultural contest that is deserving of a more elevated discourse.

The Movement of the 1960s will remain a necessary point of reference for the foreseeable future, just as one's relationship to the Old Left of the 1930s shaped the politics of the 1940s and 1950s. This is frequently not understood by conservative activists who entered the political arena in the late 1970s and in the 1980s. The result is that they do not understand where their opponents, and now a good many of their friends, are "coming from," as it used to be said. In the churches—among some evangelical and most Roman Catholic and oldline Protestant activists—the 1960s live on. In sociological terms, the churches are "soft institutions," and they have provided a haven for refugees from radicalisms past. So much is this the case that a while back *The Nation*, the flagship journal of the American left, declared that the religious left is the only left left.

There is a large measure of truth in that. But history is change as well as continuity, and it seems improbable that the language and imperatives of justice will for long be contained in their present and narrowly partisan packaging. The biblical proposition is inherently radical and seeks expression in restless discipleship. We are told that the social justice thing has been done. Others add that it has also been discredited. We do well not to believe either claim.

Until wars end and the prisoners are released, until the blind see and the hungry are fed, until the most vulnerable, the unborn, the aged, are protected, the "justice thing" will not have been done. Each generation will be renewed by the authentically radical who are at home among the wretched of the earth, who find truth along the fault lines of every social order, and who act on the promise that the dice of the Kingdom are indeed loaded on the side of those in direst need. To be sure, such radicals will from time to time find themselves part of what looks like a mass movement. But, because they are radicals, they will not count on it. And if or when it happens, they will not trust it. They will not mistake it for *the* movement of the promised Kingdom by which they are both bound and freed.

4. The Unencumbered Self and the Underclass

Now is the time to praise particularity. That is itself a general proposition, of course. But it has particular parts, both theoretical and practical. In this chapter we attend briefly to some of the theory of it, and then focus on a particular part that is most painful, the emergence of an underclass in our society, notably in black America.

In current thinking about culture and religion there is much discussion about "post-liberalism." The term is subject to sundry interpretations and may turn out to be as rubbery and confused as the "liberalism" to which it is "post." But the idea advanced by thinkers such as George Lindbeck and the late Hans Frei of Yale is that liberalism is basically an "emotive/expressive" mode of thinking in which it is assumed that different doctrines and stories are essentially expressing the same truths, only in different ways. Post-liberalism, then, is a recapturing of the importance of "cultural/linguistic traditions," of specific stories, communal memories, and even dogmas. Post-liberalism is suspicious of facile universalizations and is attached to particularities.

The advancement of the post-liberal argument is, I believe, a most promising project. It underscores the importance of *ressourcement*, of returning to the sources, in order to revitalize distinctive traditions of experience and interpretation. It accents distinctive ways of construing reality. Much of contemporary religious thought, however,

is still following in the footsteps of a liberalism that has
its intellectual origins in nineteenth-century Protestantism,
notably in post-Schleiermacher German thought.

Karl Marx punned that nobody could understand the
modern situation without going through "the fiery brook"
of Ludwig Feuerbach, whose name, of course, means fiery
brook. Much the same can be said of Friedrich Schleiermacher (d. 1834) with respect to the understanding of
religion in the modern world. One must worry about any
religious thinker who does not acknowledge a debt to
Schleiermacher—almost as much as one worries about
those who do not recognize the limits of Schleiermacher.
He set the course of "liberal" religious thought, and what
he set in motion has by no means exhausted itself. This
is dramatically evident in the case of some "progressive"
evangelical thinkers and with many influential voices in the
Roman Catholic academic theology establishment. While
the most reflective thinkers are analyzing the ways in
which it failed, that old liberalism continues to be attractive
to those who believe that they were formed (deformed) by
essentially oppressive patterns of religious thought. They
understand progress as a process of being liberated from
tradition and particularity. In some cases, it is not so much
a matter of being liberated as being able to justify the traditional and particular by appeal to allegedly universal truths.
The attraction is by no means limited to Christian thinkers.

For example, "My Memory Fails Me" is the heading of
a message from Jewish Theological Seminary (JTS) in New
York, recently printed as a full-page advertisement in the
New York Times. The point of the message is that the
distinctive memories, myths, and dogmas of a tradition
are confining. We are, JTS says, carrying around "years of
slanted, narrow memories" that distort our vision. "What
we need to do is let some of them go." We should "crack
the dogma, peel away the mythology, and trade memories."
We should listen to one another. "Maybe we ought to try
seeing as God sees, from all the angles."

It is hard to oppose the claim that we should listen to one another. It is equally hard, however, to suppose that we have much to say to one another unless we have each internalized the tradition that distinguishes our contribution to the conversation. The vaulting universalism of the JTS message seems both quaint and naive. JTS says "this message conveys the essence of our developing religious tradition." When the representatives of a tradition begin to talk about the "essence" of that tradition, they are almost surely on the way to abandoning it. So nineteenth-century liberalism spoke much about "the essence of Christianity" on the way to liberating itself from the awkward particularities of the historical reality that is Christianity.

The late Abraham Joshua Heschel, once the chief luminary of JTS, was fond of telling the story of a woman who had problems participating in the synagogue service. "The service doesn't say what I mean," she complained to the rabbi. The rabbi responded, "Madam, I am afraid you have it backward. The important thing is not that the service says what you mean. The important thing is that you mean what the service says." The JTS message about "our developing religious tradition" also seems to have it backward. The suggestion that there is available to any of us a perspective that is universal, historically unconditioned, and all-comprehensive is touchingly ingenuous. Those who "try seeing as God sees" have indeed suffered a failure of memory. Contra the JTS message, it is not the memory that fails us but we who fail the memory. The communal memory is clear enough in addressing our ambition to see as God sees: "For as the heavens are higher than the earth, so are my ways higher than your ways, and my thoughts than your thoughts" (Isaiah 55).

When we think that we can see as God sees we are in fact looking through the spectacles of the very particular, and now discredited, tradition of religious liberalism. In saying that that tradition is discredited we do not mean to say that it is dead. It has a powerful appeal for those who

are embarrassed by their particularity. It also appeals to
those who have honestly concluded that their own tradition is not rich or varied or strong enough to make sense of
the truth they have encountered in other traditions. And it
appeals to people who do not know how to cope with
pluralism. Their response to pluralism is an attempt to
transcend the particular in order to embrace the universal.
But that response to pluralism is a denial of pluralism. It
results in a monism of indifference, of pretending that our
deepest differences make no difference. Genuine pluralism
is the vibrant engagement of differences, in the confidence
that we are ultimately held together by the One Who alone
sees as God sees. Namely God.

A more humane world is a world that is safe for difference. Nothing so well demonstrates the truth that traveling
narrows the mind as the number of visitors to antique or
hostile lands who return to proclaim their discovery that
the people there are just like us. To be sure, likenesses
should not be denied. But neither can they support sweep-
ing affirmations about, for instance, universal needs and
entitlements. The likenesses that are most believable are
either animal or metaphysical. We human beings are much
alike in terms of animal needs, and we are all—or so most
of us think—children of God. But such equalities are in
the one case so basic and in the other so elevated as to
have little bearing on the way we decide how to order our
relations with one another.

Difference, not equality, is both the spice of life and
the stuff of political morality. Nobody prizes his equality,
except the person who has previously been deprived and
views equality as a transitional point on the way to becoming different in a way he considers superior. What makes
life precious is difference, not equality; particularity, not
universality. We do not identify ourselves as human beings first, but as sons and daughters, fathers and mothers,
tribesmen and neighbors, Christians and Jews, brokers and
writers, and supporters of the Baltimore Orioles. We thus

frequently feel put upon by the necessarily generalized rules of the political order because we are none of us people-in-general.

This is powerfully demonstrated in *King Lear*. Recall Goneril and Regan, the dreadful daughters, who are going back on the agreement that Lear should after his abdication go about with a retinue of knights. The daughters contend that they have knights enough to provide him company and protection, and he therefore has no need for a retinue of his own. To which Lear responds: "O, reason not the need! Our basest beggars / Are in the poorest things superfluous. / Allow not nature more than nature needs, / Man's life is cheap as beast's." To "reason the need" is to ignore the difference between kingly Lear and any vagrant out on the heath. To give to each according to his need, rather than according to his due, is to reduce all to the base equality of animal being. Civilization consists in the construction of distinctions to which attention must be paid. Arthur Miller did not get it quite right. Attention must be paid Willy Loman, not first because "he's a human being," but because he is the myriad specifics that make him Willy Loman.

At last, out on the heath with Kent, the Fool, and the mad beggar Poor Tom, Lear descends to the final equality of basic need. Abandoning verse, he speaks the prosaic truth: "Is man no more than this? Consider him well. Thou owest the worm no silk, the beast no hide, the sheep no wool, the cat no perfume. Ha! here's three on's are sophisticated! Thou art the thing itself; unaccommodated man is no more but such a poor, bare, forked animal as thou art." To unaccommodated man, to the thing itself, nothing is due. True, he is still accommodated by the claim that he is a child of God. But that only makes him equal, on a par with all who are children of God; and nobody loves or respects humanity, moralisms to the contrary notwithstanding. That metaphysical equality means, as Miller says, that Willy Loman must not be treated like a dog, but that is a long way from treating Willy Loman like Willy Loman. In addition, many do not accept the metaphysical claim that people are children of God, a claim that checks our propensity for treating people like dogs.

For most political purposes, our dignity is in our difference. This has been well understood by the masters of gulags and concentration camps. Stripping people of their social particularities—of their relationships, property, and even their names—they reduce them to "the thing itself." A species of liberal sentimentality asserts that the social and historical are mere accretions. Beneath such accidentals, it is said, are the "natural rights of man." But beneath the social and historical there is nothing at all, except the theological claim to dignity—a claim that carries no weight with the godless. Our differences of family, tribe, nation, religion, achievement, and privilege are both safety and danger. They constitute the lines of frequent conflict, but also the lines along which can be built the institutions of protection and respect.

Such institutions are the genius of the republican form of democratic governance. To make the world safe for such democracy is to make the world safe for difference. Contra the aforementioned and well-intentioned travelers, a more humane society and a more peaceful world require a broadening of the mind to embrace the truth that "they" are not just like us.

Among those in America who are emphatically *not* just like us ("us" being people who read and write books such as this) are the people to be found in what is now called the black underclass. The term underclass is somewhat analogous to the Marxist idea of the *lumpenproletariat.* It is a class of people who are under, apart from, the operative classes in a society. Put differently, they are the people who are not part of the cultural, social, and economic circulatory system of the society. They are, in the words of sociologist William Julius Wilson, the "radically isolated."

Here, too, attention must be paid the particulars. Generalities such as "black America" or even "the black underclass" are, for me, inevitably made specific by the people of St. John the Evangelist. Straddling the Williamsburg and Bedford-Stuyvesant sections of Brooklyn, that parish was for seventeen years the site of a ministry of unrivaled satisfactions. It was about as close to happiness as one is likely to experience this side of the Kingdom. But what about those people of Brooklyn, then and now? It is a question often asked, and the usual answer goes something like this: By any material measure, the people of that community are better off now than they were thirty years ago. And yet the conclusion is irresistible that they are, all in all, worse off. Reasoning the need, as Lear put it, there are needs being met now that were not met then. But there is less happiness.

The material factors are easily reasoned. Today there is more money, considerably more money. A combination of welfare, the underground economy, and crime (mainly in drug dealing) sees to that. The things that money can buy—cars, televisions, gadgets, and airline tickets to visit distant places—are in ample evidence. Thirty years ago one encountered children who were hungry simply because there was not money to buy food. Today some children still go hungry, because money is squandered or because parents don't care or because they are otherwise preoccupied in their pharmaceutical wonderlands. Most heartwrenching are the children born addicted to drugs or diseased with AIDS. There are hungry children, but not, or at least not significantly, because there is no money. The nonmaterial factors, however, are harder to reason and harder to measure—and so much more important in determining that elusive reality called "quality of life."

Thirty years ago there was the civil rights movement—meaning, above all, Dr. King and his dream—and it generated a powerful sense of hopefulness. The evidence seemed palpable that a new world was indeed adawning; one could smell hope in the air. Those who had been shut out were now to be let in. And coming into the society's common home, they would make it a warmer and better place. It was not simply hopefulness about the condition of black Americans; it was hopefulness about the American experiment and blacks as an agent of its redemption. During the years of Lyndon Johnson there was the War on Poverty with all its vaulting promises. I was involved then in dispensing millions of dollars to programs that were geared to the goal of "maximum feasible participation of the poor."

We were sometimes asked whether all the money was accounted for and well used. A common and too facile answer was: Not all of it, but if some is misappropriated, that only means that poor people are being given a chance to get in on the general corruption of "the system." Today it is evident that that corruption contributed to producing cruel consequences for the very people who presumably were being helped. There is no denying that an element of cynicism came with the rush of government money. Many young men and women got into "the poverty business," moving from the mean streets to government-funded office suites almost overnight. The impression was given that this is the way to succeed in America, organizing "grassroots" political power to demand ever bigger pieces of the government handout. In fact, one did not have to do much in the way of demanding. At least for several years, the federal dispensary was almost desperately looking around for organizations to give money to.

Not surprisingly, community organizations of amazing variety quickly appeared, giving rise to a class of entrepreneurs who would come to be called, often unfairly, "poverty pimps." The designers of the War on Poverty were, I believe, sincere in their intention to attend to the particularities of people and institutions in poor communities. They did not intend to design social policy "as the crow flies" (Michael Oakeshott). They wanted to meet people where they are, as it was said. "Maximum feasible participation of the poor" was, for the most part, well intended, but some years later, Daniel Patrick (now Senator) Moynihan would describe the politics of the war on poverty in a book titled *Maximum Feasible Misunderstanding.*[1]

Perhaps inevitably, government programs tended to weaken rather than strengthen the "infrastructure" of poor communities. The infrastructure consists of what Peter Berger and I described as the "mediating structures" of society—the face-to-face and people-to-people institutions such as family, church, neighborhood organization, and innumerable voluntary associations.[2] (In 1989, President Bush would refer to the mediating structures as "a thousand points of light," and his domestic policy advisers dubbed this approach as the "New Paradigm.") The mediating structures approach is comprehensive, suggesting new directions for social policy in areas as diverse as education, health care, housing, and criminal justice. Whether the Bush administration, or any other administration, has the nerve and wit to advance the implementation of this approach is quite another question.

In the old anti-poverty programs the infrastructure was weakened because, human nature being as it is, power and influence follow the money. The money was coming from Washington and, even though there were numerous state and local conduits, and even though efforts were made to locate decision making as close to "the people" as possible, nobody could forget for long the location of the font of fiscal blessings. In our research projects on mediating structures, Berger and I employed what we called the minimal proposition and the maximal proposition. The minimal proposition is that public policy should be designed to do as little damage as possible to the mediating structures. The maximal proposition is that public policy should utilize mediating structures as much as possible. We are much more confident of the minimal than of the maximal proposition. The various anti-poverty programs tended to use (in the pejorative sense of "use") mediating structures in a way that left them feeling demoralized and, indeed, used. Particularly hard hit in this respect were the black churches—the most important mediating structure next to the family in the communities that the war on poverty was intended to help.

The realities of the black underclass, what is happening in the lives of real people, are clearly and poignantly detailed in works such as William Julius Wilson's *The Truly Disadvantaged*.[3] Here is demonstrated the atomization of individuals, of people who become, in Michael Sandel's term, "unencumbered selves." No longer encumbered or clothed by the particularities of communities of memory and mutual obligation, they stand, like Poor Tom in *Lear*, naked to the world. It is a serious disservice to our understanding, and to these people, to offer the superficial explanation that their plight is due to racism. William Julius Wilson saw this some years ago. A black sociologist at the University of Chicago, Wilson was much pilloried when, in 1978, he wrote on "the declining significance of race." His argument was that racial discrimination was a fast diminishing factor in explaining the problems experienced by poor black people (meaning, roughly, the bottom third of black America). Of course, this threatened the orthodoxy of those who simply *know* that the plight of blacks is attributable to ours being a racist society, and the relevant data on racial attitudes be damned.

A caring analysis that cares enough to be careful suggests problems even more deeply troubling than those suggested by facile formulas about racism. Consider but one item. In 1990 in Bedford-Stuyvesant, the largest black section of New York City, the City Department of Health reported that 83 percent of all children born were born to women outside wedlock. In the great majority of cases, they were born to women who are without men who accept responsibility for their children. Without fathers, in the ordinary sense of that term. What is true of Bedford-Stuyvesant is true of the black underclass nationally. Millions of children do not know, and will never know, what it means to have a father. More poignantly, they do not know what a father is. They do not know anyone who has a father or is a father. They do not know adult males who accept open-ended responsibility for their progeny.

Of course, this did not just happen last year. It has been happening for close to thirty years. It takes little imagination to begin to understand the intergenerational consequences of this nightmare. We might reasonably ask whether, in all of human history, we can find an instance of a large population group in which the institution of the family simply disappeared. The question is reasonable and ominous, for the answer is almost certainly no. There is, therefore, no historical precedent supporting the hope that the family, once it has disappeared, can be reconstituted.

Add to this the dramatic rise in crime—especially violent crime and violent crime overwhelmingly by blacks against blacks—plus a pervasive sense of helplessness and hopelessness, and it becomes evident why I believe that the people of St. John the Evangelist were better off in 1961. Wilson argues, correctly I think, that a new and deeply troubling factor is the "radical isolation" of the black underclass. Thirty or fifty years ago, black communities typically included a middle class, people on their way to becoming middle class, and even a significant number of the well-to-do. Not today. The top third, composed of economically successful blacks, has long since moved out of "the ghetto," as have most of the middle third who are making their way much as most whites are in "the system." True, on the edges of black areas such as Harlem and Bedford-Stuyvesant, there are "strivers' rows" where some of the well-to-do still live. But those sections are as self-consciously isolated and demarcated street by street as is any division between black and white neighborhoods on the west side of Chicago. Additionally galling to the poor is the further demarcation between "American" and "Island" blacks. The latter are from the Carribean and, being notably more successful in the American context, they make it clear that they do not wish to be associated with "them."

These dramatic variations within communities of the same color make it impossible to explain the black underclass simply in terms of racial discrimination. The grim fact is that we have left in the hard-core inner cities large populations of the endemically dependent poor, without the stability, example, and reasons for hope supplied by those whose lives are in working order. Wilson and others recognize that the law of unintended consequences is hard at work here. Blacks who are making it made their way out of the ghetto in large part because of the enormous achievements, legal and otherwise, in reducing racial discrimination in housing and employment. The answer, obviously, is not to reinstitute racial discrimination. Some partial answers may be found by facing up to the realities of the radically isolated black underclass.

Part of what is meant by radical isolation is that the black underclass becomes increasingly forgettable for many Americans. In a city such as New York, this is depicted with both hilarity and pathos in Tom Wolfe's *The Bonfire of the Vanities*. But for the great majority of Americans the underclass is much more forgettable than it is for Mr. Wolfe's "Masters of the Universe" who live in their sumptuous apartments on Park Avenue. Even the most advantaged New Yorker is daily reminded by the street life of drug addicts, pushers, prostitutes, and general wanderers that there is something terribly out of whack in the societal order. Most Americans, as New Yorkers must ever be reminded, do not live in New York—or any place like New York. Despite all the talk about the rapid urbanization of America, somewhat less than 10 percent of the population lives in cities of a million or more. In fact, the black underclass comprises only 3 or 4 percent of the American population and is highly concentrated. Little wonder that most Americans find the problem eminently forgettable.

This is not to say that there are not parties concerned about the problem—in universities, churches, and political offices. There are, and they are right in relentlessly focusing attention on the poor in our society. Many of them are wrong, however, when they suggest that the homeless and the underclass are typical of, or are the inevitable consequence of, the American "system." It is equally wrong, I am persuaded for reasons that cannot delay us here, to perpetuate the discredited doctrine that the answer to poverty is a more egalitarian distribution of the wealth. The answer is more effectively to incorporate people into the circulatory system of the society, including productive economic activity. Since the doctrines of redistribution have been discredited, and since we are uncertain about how to go about incorporation of the poor, it is understandable that we are inclined to forget the poor. It may be, as is commonly charged, that Americans are suffering from "compassion fatigue." It is at least equally true that Americans are less credulous about what can be done about or for the very poor, and especially about what government can do. And yet it is certainly right to refuse to let the forgettable be forgotten. The nature of a society is measured not only by its achievements, but also along its fault lines. And there is, in the biblical view of things, a most particular interest in those living along the fault lines.

Since conventional ideas about racism and wealth redistribution are of little use, and may indeed be more misleading than illuminating, we need to think anew. To be sure, we may convince ourselves that we do not need to think at all about the underclass. Most Americans are physically distant from these problems, and the more advantaged who live in large cities can, through prudence and private security systems, isolate themselves from the radically isolated. But to resign ourselves to a permanent underclass that lives in abject dependency on the dole and is kept

behind ever higher barricades in order to protect the rest
of the population is, quite simply, morally unacceptable. It
is unacceptable because of what it does to people in the
underclass who turn upon one another in violent excretion
of their self-contempt. And it is unacceptable because, for
the good of the entire society, we should not be prepared
to go along with the idea that our way of life is compati-
ble with, maybe even requires, millions of fellow citizens
remaining outside the spheres of achievement and hope.

And so we must think anew. We do well to recall the
words of Lincoln in the face of the greatest conflict in our
national history: "The dogmas of the quiet past are inadequate to the stormy present. The occasion is piled high
with difficulty, and we must rise with the occasion. As our
case is new, so we must think anew and act anew. We must
disenthrall ourselves, and then we shall save our country."
New thinking may come from unexpected sources. Since
the New Deal, it has been assumed that "liberals" cared
about the poor, while "conservatives" were either indifferent or hostile to their interests. Now, in the last decade
and more, signs abound that that is changing. It is terribly
important that it change, especially if those analysts are
right who discern a growing conservatism among American young people. Of course, as that change progresses, it
will become increasingly difficult to distinguish liberal and
conservative, which may be all to the good.

New thinking is represented by, for instance, Charles
Murray, who is usually described as a conservative intellectual. Murray is something of an iconoclast, and his work
has generated understandable controversy. Many people,
including this writer, are made nervous by, for instance,
his work on race differences in intelligence and social
competence. But it may be that we cannot "disenthrall
ourselves" of old dogmas without offending against en-
trenched societal taboos. In any event, Murray's *Losing
Ground* made an invaluable contribution by putting numbers and clear theory on the widespread intuition that

anti-poverty programs of the past had been radically mis-conceived. Similarly, his later work, *In Pursuit of Happiness and Good Government*, forced many people to go back to square one in thinking about what we intend to accomplish in public policy.[4]

As a social analyst, Murray is more a radical than a conservative in the relentless attention he pays to what is actually happening in the lives of real people, and in letting the evidence take him where it will. As he explores alternative social policies, he invites us to engage in "thought experiments," experiments that defy conventional categories of political persuasion. Although he has well-justified doubts about John Rawls's famous "difference principle" that is designed to keep attention focused on the least advantaged, it is always the least advantaged that we are to keep in mind. Thus, for example, Murray and others argue for increasing choice in education through vouchers or other means, and make the case that such a change would be to the advantage of the children of the underclass—including those who might stay in public schools. That argument is important, because the defenders of the status quo who oppose educational choice conventionally claim that poor children would be the losers if parents had a greater say in schooling.

One of the more encouraging signs in this last decade of the century is that many Americans are beginning to disenthrall themselves of a long-standing captivity to the notion that government schools should have a monopoly on public funding. Even more conventionally liberal organizations, such as the Brookings Institute, are issuing studies that advocate the advancement of public purpose through public support for non-governmental agencies in education. This is a historic change, for the paradigm of the "common school" movement launched in the early part of the last century has held our public policy thinking in thrall far too long. There are many arguments for educational choice, not the least being that it would create space for the free exercise of religious and other important diversities in American life. In the present context, however, we should recognize its high promise for the underclass. To involve parents and mediating institutions in the choices *and responsibilities* of something so basic as education is, at a point of great social and psychological moment, to draw them out of radical isolation.

Anticipating an obvious objection, we should readily acknowledge that educational choice is no panacea. Panacean remedies are not available to us. Nobody is entirely sure about all the causes that went into the creation of what is called the underclass, and the remedies remain similarly unsure. As skeptical as we should be when people tell us a situation is unprecedented, there are, as we have seen, important respects in which this situation does indeed seem to be unprecedented. There are no guaranteed alternatives to the destructive policies of past and present. There is the imperative to think anew. We can replace a form of policy analysis that focuses on social engineering and aggregate results with an approach that emphasizes, in the words of Murray, "enabling conditions for the pursuit of happiness." Government policies cannot provide happiness and well being; they might be able to contribute to the conditions in which people can better pursue these goods.

Most people, whether advantaged or disadvantaged, are the best experts on what is good for them. That proposition is no mere platitude. We can all think immediately of so many exceptions to the rule that the rule is thrown into question. Many years ago, Edward Banfield wrote in *The Unheavenly City*[5] that 6 percent of the members of any society will be unsocializable, simply unable to cope. Some are severely handicapped, physically or mentally; others are incorrigibly lazy or prone to criminal behavior; yet others, whom we may think quite sane in most respects, will simply decide that they do not want to "fit" in the society in which they find themselves.

We can quibble over Banfield's 6 percent. Maybe it is only 3 percent. But a moment's thought about any small town or large city of our acquaintance will bear out the observation that a substantial number of people are not going to be socialized in ways that the rest of the population considers "normal." If the lower percentage is right, in a town of ten thousand there will be three hundred people unable to cope without intensive help from others; in a country such as the United States, we are speaking about approximately six million people. Again, the precise percentage is not crucial. Make it even a very unrealistic one percent, and it is apparent that scale does not change the substantive problem.

Of course not all who are "socially incompetent" are in the underclass, not by a long shot. But many of them are. The underclass is the most concentrated population of those who cannot or will not cope when it comes to family responsibility, education, work, and living within the criminal law. Nor, it is important to note, is everyone in the underclass black. There is a proportionately significant number of Hispanics (notably Puerto Ricans), and a significant number of whites. But again, the population most significantly concentrated—in terms of both numbers and consequence for the entire society—is the black underclass.

A free society is one that creates as much space as possible for the "abnormal" in social behavior. But it must always strive to do so in a way that does not destroy the norms that constitute the "normal." That we have in our society severely weakened assumptions about normality is indicated by the convention of putting "normal" and "abnormal" within quotation marks. That normality has become a suspect category is an ambiguous, but perhaps unavoidable, result of our generally laudable desire to be "inclusive" and sensitive to diversity. After all, some of those people who do not "fit in" may be talking with angels. Most of us have been struck at one time or another with the thought that those who are called crazy may really be the sane ones, and our normality is the true madness. As healthy, and humbling, as it may be for us to entertain that hypothesis, however, no society can accept it as a working premise.

While we should want to maintain as much free space as possible for aberrant behavior, there are numerous instances in which intervention is necessary, especially when people might do grave damage to themselves or others. In such cases, if we understand the importance of particularities in human life, social policy should encourage interventions of caring and damage-control by those who are closest to the people in need of help. Here again, mediating structures are critical. The "minimal proposition" mentioned above is based upon the fact that, in everyday behavior, the great bulk of such needs are indeed met by families, support groups, and other voluntary associations. Policies should be designed to encourage, and never to discourage, that pattern of caring. Advocates of expanded government programs routinely point out that it exacts a great sacrifice for families to take care of, for instance, the aged and mentally and physically handicapped. The curious thing in our culture is that self-sacrifice, caring for someone else at the price of our own "self-actualization," is thought to be a problem to be solved rather than a virtue to be cultivated. Fortunately, that is not true of the entire culture, but is a belief chiefly located in leadership sectors that, for various reasons, favor expanded government care and control.

I say "for various reasons," and it must be acknowledged that some of those reasons are indeed benign. Anyone looking at all the people in our society who are in deep trouble is understandably moved to say, "Somebody should do something about this." Guided by the dominant social policy paradigms of the last several decades, that "somebody" turns out to be the government. Or, as frequently, it is said that "we" should do something, assuming that "we" means the collective we of state action. These are the social policy paradigms from which we must disenthrall ourselves. First by creating greater free space for aberrant behavior, and, second, by encouraging intervention, where intervention is necessary, by those persons and mediating institutions that provide identity and a sense of personal narrative, thus clothing the naked selves in need of help.

All this said, it is likely that there will always be a residual need for social policies of state intervention. Such interventions should be viewed as a last resort rather than, as is too often the case at present, a first resort. In connection with the underclass we need to think anew about what we call welfare policies. Here another rule comes into play: *Policies should be premised not on pathologies but on potentialities.* That is to say, it should not be assumed that everyone in the underclass is "socially incompetent" or is permanently dependent. One can readily understand why social policy thinking is focused on pathologies. After all, the people in the most desperate situation naturally attract the greater measure of sympathetic attention. But if in our thinking we put the most desperate people front center stage, we will likely increase the number of people who are desperate.

In other words, social policies premised upon pathologies result in multiplying the pathologies we would remedy. This is the bind we find ourselves in when we reward (financially or otherwise) people who are below a certain income level or who engage in aberrant behavior (criminal or otherwise). The bind is dismally evident when we create "entitlement" categories that encourage people to stay in the categories to which benefits are attached. One mistake we can make in thinking about this problem is to assume that the poor and disadvantaged are, day-by-day, carefully calculating how to get the maximum number of benefits from the welfare state. Many of them are so radically isolated from reality, so "out of it," that such rational calculation is entirely beyond them. It is equally a mistake and an ugly form of condescension, however, to assume that poor people are stupid. Although they perhaps do not do so with a bookkeeper's precision, most people have a roughly serviceable idea of the connection between behavior and rewards.

We are speaking, of course, about incentives and disincentives. (The experts in the field talk about perverse incentive structures, which is not a bad way of putting it.) Social policy premised upon pathology tends to reward pathology. Social policy premised upon potentiality tends to reward the realization of potentiality. In the latter approach, the focus is on the good that might happen rather than the bad that has happened. That might sound like naive optimism to people who are engaged in the immediate urgencies of trying to cope with the problems of people who find themselves in situations resulting from the bad things that have in fact happened. Undoubtedly, there will always be a need for the rescue operations, the band-aid measures, and the hand-outs to help people get through the day. But we are here discussing the paradigms by which we might think anew about what we are trying to do in social policy.

To understand the difference between policy premised upon potentiality rather than pathology, consider some of our most basic ways of thinking about poverty. Most of us are conditioned to think that poverty is the surprising, the puzzling, thing. That is, in part, because most of us are not poor, and we think that not being poor is the "normal" thing. If, however, we survey human history, and even our world today, it becomes obvious that what we call poverty has been the normal thing. Poverty is not the "problem" in the sense of its being puzzling. The puzzling thing is why so many people are not poor. Put differently, what we need better to understand is not why some people are poor but why so many people participate in and benefit from the production of wealth.

In recent decades we have had studies beyond numbering that try to figure out the "causes of poverty." For many years, it seemed that such a study was showing up on my desk almost every second day. No doubt the intentions behind these studies are good, but one cannot shake the impression that they are getting things backwards. If we ever got the absolutely definitive study on the causes of poverty, what would we have learned? We would have learned how to cause poverty. Presumably, no one is interested in doing that. We want to learn, rather, how to cause wealth—or, better, how to help people enter into the economic circulatory system of the society. In our entirely proper, indeed imperative, worrying about the underclass, for example, we should want to know why two thirds of our black fellow citizens are *not* in the underclass.

At one level, the answers would seem to be very simple. Numerous studies have indicated, for instance, that there are some very basic, almost embarrassingly basic, factors that make it highly predictable whether someone will or will not end up in the underclass. If, for example, a young person finishes high school, gets an entry level job and stays employed for three years, and gets married, there is a 98 percent chance that he or she will not live in poverty. Just those three simple conditions, and yet how difficult it is to understand all the factors that go into the fulfillment of those three conditions. There is probably little that public policy can do to affect those many factors one way or another. We have already mentioned the growing support for one public policy reform, using vouchers and similar mechanisms to make schools accountable to parents and communities. But the education factor is only one of many. The factors conducive to living a life of productive citizenship probably have more to do with culture than with public policy.

Culture is, among other things, the available ideas by which people understand themselves and try to make sense of their lives. In recent decades, both elite and popular cultures have disseminated ideas that have made it more difficult for young blacks, among others, to enter into the societal mainstream. In the slick magazines and big name talk shows, for example, drugs were for a long time celebrated as chic. Marriage and family life were depicted as vestiges of an oppressive past, and "going it alone" was portrayed as the route of self-fulfillment for women. Surely the ready availability of abortion made it easier for young men to shrug off responsibility for their sexual behavior, since it was so easy to tell the woman (often only a teenager) to have "her" problem taken care of.

It is true that many of the ideas and behaviors associated with a "liberated lifestyle" are no longer so fashionable. On the talk shows now, it is common to hear the trend-setters talk about drug-free living and the importance of marriage and family. It is not uncommon to hear a good word said even for chastity. The trend-setters are usually in an economic and social position to learn from their mistakes and put their lives back in order. The poor, and especially the young among the poor, were walking a tightrope to begin with. For them, the "alternative lifestyles" that were hawked by the fashionable turned out to be alternatives to a sustainable life. Part of the tragic truth about the underclass is that these people are now paying the price of having listened to those who are, presumably, their social betters.

Among the more pernicious ideas floating in the cultural ether, and especially through the airwaves, are ideas that encourage young blacks to believe that they are victims of "the system." Those who disseminate these ideas typically think of themselves as compassionate, but surely there can be nothing more cruel than to tell young blacks that they are no more than ciphers, products of other people's behavior, powerless to change their lives unless "the system" is changed.

We are talking here about Michael Walker of Maujer Street, Brooklyn, and all the other Michael Walkers of America. Our point is that Michael should be encouraged to assume responsibility for his life, but it is also more than that. The point is that it should *not* be suggested to him that his behavior, and the consequent course of his life, is contingent upon two hundred million non-black Americans changing their putatively racist ways. Michael is eighteen, out of school, on drugs, has fathered two children to whom he is not a father, has done a short stretch in jail, and lives off a combination of his girlfriends' welfare checks and petty crime. He is told by people of prominence, including some called civil rights leaders, that the situation in which he finds himself is the result of "the system." The system in question is variously described in terms of white racism, capitalism, political corruption, or some other abstraction quite beyond Michael Walker's control. If he believes this description—and after all, it is offered to him by people in positions of moral authority, including religious leaders—what is he to do about it? The answer is that he can indulge in revolutionary fantasies, take out his anger on those nearest to him, or despair. His life will, as likely as not, be contorted by all three of these responses, and perhaps by others equally negative. The language of victimhood and systemic oppression is usually associated with what is called the politics of compassion. Viewed from the perspective of those at the bottom of society, it is the politics of cruel, if unintended, consequences.

We have it on the very highest authority that the poor we will have with us always. But we have not always had with us, and we need not always have with us, the present distress of the black underclass. And, as much as we might want to forget them, they are with us. Other people no doubt have other experiences that keep that reality in mind as they think about the kind of society we are and might be. For this writer, it is the ever-present awareness of the people of St. John the Evangelist in Brooklyn, then and now. It is the Michael Walkers and the Cheryl Johnsons, and the children of the children who do not know what it is to have a father, who do not know what a father is.

And so we stumble upon Poor Tom on the heath of our inner cities. Here is Sandel's "unencumbered self," and Lear's "unaccommodated man." "Reason not the need," said Lear. In our social policies aimed at the poor, policies supported by the best and the brightest in our universities and churches, we reasoned the need. In the form of things that can be counted and calculated, many needs were reasoned and, in fact, met. Income redistribution systems, through welfare and entitlement programs, were put in place and, much partisan political rhetoric to the contrary, have for the most part been kept in place. Similarly, systems for the "delivery" of social services are in place. But the most important things needed by persons in society cannot be delivered. Education cannot be delivered. Family cannot be delivered. The mediating institutions, the communities of memory and mutual aid, cannot be delivered.

Twenty-five years ago, the waggish Pat Moynihan observed that the main reason poor people are poor is that they do not have enough money. Many smiled and nodded assent to the apparently unarguable. Now we know better. But old ideas die hard. Those who resist thinking anew cling to the paradigms of increased wealth redistribution and expanded delivery systems. To abandon those paradigms, they fear, means letting America off the hook. The post-liberal argument of this chapter, however, lets nobody off the hook. It does not let us off the hook in terms of redesigning social policies—policies that may cost as much or more, also in dollars, than those we have now—that encourage people to be their better selves, that empower the underclass to break out of its captivity to powerless dependency. More demandingly, it does not let the rest of us off the hook in terms of reviving among ourselves the communities of virtue and obligation that alone prevent the false liberations of the autonomous self from turning all of us into what Lear called "the thing itself."

5. A Tale of Heroism
and Horror

"My father said the whole world is one big chain. One little part breaks and the chain is broken and it won't work anymore." These are the words of Johan, a German who in 1941 at age seventeen became a rescuer of Jews from Hitler's Final Solution. In our time of moral flaccidity and confusion, we need to understand why such people did what they did. There are studies that help us toward that end, such as *The Altruistic Personality* by Samuel and Pearl Oliner.[1] The more than seven hundred rescuers interviewed in depth by the Oliners and their colleagues had in common that they wanted the world to work again, and to work morally. They were convinced of the truth that each had an obligation to keep the chain together, and to do what they could to mend it where it was broken.

The image of a chain is apt. One is bound and held captive by a chain. A chain suggests a matter not of choice but of duty. What the rescuers did was a matter of ultimate duty, one might say of religious duty. Here, of course, one thinks of religion as its meaning is derived from *religare*, to bind together, as with a chain. Because the rescuers knew themselves to be so bound, they evidenced a remarkable freedom, including the freedom to act to free others from the horror of the Holocaust. The people studied in *The Altruistic Personality* and related literature illumine the seeming paradox of freedom through obligation.

There is no agreement on the number of rescuers of Jews under the Third Reich. Some scholars say 50,000, others so many as 500,000. Obviously, different definitions of a rescuer are in play here. The Oliners estimate that for everyone whom they count as a rescuer there were ten others who were more or less supportive in helping the rescuers to do what they did. Add to this the number of people who knew what was going on and "helped" by not informing the authorities and it becomes apparent that millions of Germans and of others in German-occupied territories opposed, at greater and lesser degrees of risk, the Reich's program for resolving "the Jewish question." And yet, all these people are a small fraction of those who could have helped. We should try to understand why those who did help did what they did.

Books on the Holocaust typically focus on "the problem of evil." It is as important to understand the possibility of good. Exploring that possiblity does not blunt the edge of evil. Far from denying or diluting the evil, the story of the rescuers throws it into sharpest relief. The horror was not inevitable or irresistible. Tellings of the story of the Holocaust that attempt to "explain" it by reference to deterministic dynamics of one sort or another rob the story of its moral significance. That the horror was not necessary is evidenced by those who, at the heart of the horror, enacted the word of conscience, the simple word that is No. In this way they expose the easy lies that smooth the way of complicity with evil. To those who plead that they had no choice, the witness of the rescuers stands in clear rebuke.

There are writers in ethics and moral philosophy who are, understandably, made uneasy by the witness of the rescuers. There are self-described "realists" who systematically assault every form of "sentimentalism" that would diminish the starkness of a Hobbesian world of " a war of all against all." The possibility of human goodness threatens a moral theory that confuses realism with cynicism, and ends up by embracing a view of human behavior that is profoundly unrealistic. The concept of selfless behavior has no place in this view; it is but the product of the naive self-indulgence of a delusory "idealism."

This species of ethical theory becomes more pernicious when, by definition, all selflessness is turned into selfishness. Thus someone who behaves altruistically because he says he must be "true to himself" is, in fact, serving his self. And, it is said, this is the case even if the truth that the individual has internalized in his self is presumably derived from some source other than the self. So, for example, Jesus, in going to the cross in obedience to the Father, was being true to his self and, therefore, engaged in selfish behavior. Such definitional introversion results in a moral solipsism that is the death of moral deliberation. It need not delay us here, but it does alert us to why many resist serious reflection on human goodness as evidenced in the altruistic personality.

Fortunately, we do not have to choose between "idealists" who are blind to the dynamics of selfishness and "realists" who are blind to everything but selfishness. The human reality is more complicated, and far more interesting, than either party suggests. Yet others, however, will resist an impartial examination of the story of the rescuers for other reasons. Those reasons have to do with what might be called the hermeneutics of the Holocaust. What are the rules for interpreting the Holocaust, and who sets those rules?

There is a school that insists that the victims have a monopoly on interpretation. Others go further and claim that only the Jewish victims may be permitted to speak—a claim that is strongly resisted by those who would give voice to the millions of non-Jewish victims of the Nazi horror. On the one hand, we must maintain the particularity of the Holocaust, especially its Jewish particularity. But the Holocaust is more than another horror story, even if the premier horror story. It is more than the Jewish horror story that must take its place in a long history of horror stories about what happened to particular peoples under particular circumstances now increasingly far removed in time. It is unseemly, and a trivializing of moral reflection, when victims vie with one another in exhibiting their wounds.

Understandably, indeed necessarily, communities of particular memory will keep their stories alive, however. The sharp edge of particularity, carefully honed by the living witness of survivors, must be maintained. The stories should not be falsely universalized and collapsed into familiar generalizations about the human condition. At the same time, the hermeneutics of the Holocaust must not so pit the particular against the universal that general truths are lost. If the Holocaust is displayed as the story of the terrible things that were done to Jews, and is exploited in order to extract from non-Jews expressions of guilt and reparations in the form of, for instance, support for Israel, it will soon wear thin. Indeed it is inevitable that it wears thinner with each passing year. This is well understood by more reflective Jewish thinkers today. The Holocaust is not merely a tribal tale of woe, nor is it an instrument to be employed in gaining advantage against others. It is a particular that illuminates the general, and binds us—notably Jews and Christians—in an ever deeper examination of the sources of good and evil that shape our life together.

For people in the contemporary West, the Holocaust is perhaps the only culturally available story of absolute evil. The almost unanimous agreement on the evil of the Holocaust makes it, in its perversity, a cultural icon of incalculable value. For Christians, to be sure, the cross of Christ, humanity's attempt to obliterate God's presence among us, is the icon of absolute evil, inseparably joined to the triumph of absolute good in the resurrection. But, unlike the Holocaust, the cross will not serve for public purposes. For Christians, it portrays the cruciform shape of all history, personal and public, short of the final consummation. It is the deepest, the richest, and the most true portrayal of reality. But it divides Christians and Jews. To Jews it remains a stumbling block, as it is also foolishness to others who do not recognize its truth (1 Corinthians 1:23). According to the New Testament, the cross is the hidden wisdom of God, evident now to those who believe, and only in the Endtime evident to all. It should not be pressed into public service in a world that is the field where wheat and tares, faith and unfaith, must coexist until the final harvest (Matthew 13:29).

In this historical moment that is penultimate, we rely upon other intimations of ultimate good and evil. One may argue that, even in the modern era, there are other horrors that may serve as well as the Holocaust. The modern era is rich in horrors that demonstrate the world not working, the chain of caring broken. Consider the Gulag Archipelago under Stalin and his immediate successors, or Mao's Cultural Revolution, or the Cambodian genocide under Pol Pot, or the politically forced starvation of the multitudes in Ethiopia and the Sudan. It is a dismal mark of our time that other examples leap to mind, so that we can almost pick at random. Horrors vie with horrors, and scholars dispute among themselves about which are the greater. Did Stalin kill forty million or seventy million of his own citizens? The more amiable students of the subject are prepared to split the difference. The horrors of our epoch are such that, in this instance or that, we readily give or take a million—or two, or three, or more—in estimating the toll in human lives. We lost count a long time ago, and therefore the believers among us count on the counting of the One on whom no sparrow's fall is lost.

Among the horrors, however, the Holocaust is singular for a number of reasons. We know a great deal about other horrors. The work of Aleksandr Solzhenitsyn on the Gulag, for example, will stand out as a monumental achievement in modern historiography. But the literature on all the other horrors combined is small by comparison with the literature on the Holocaust. Living Judaism—the tradition of those sometimes called the People of the Book—is a tradition of books beyond numbering. And not only books, of course, but movies, documentaries, and every other available means of communication. There is another difference, too. The other horrors, unlike the Holocaust, did not happen within what is commonly understood to be "our" history of the modern West. It can be objected that National Socialism is not "our" history, that it was a clear and brutal rejection of Western civilization, and most specifically of Christian civilization. The objection is valid, of course, but then it must be added that that rejection of the West happened within the West. It perhaps was, in ways that we may never understand fully, a product of the West, just as it may be argued that radical secularization is a product of Christianity. These questions cannot be explored in detail here, but suffice it that anyone who identifies at all with our civilizational story recognizes that the Holocaust is part of "our" history in a way that, say, the bloody madness of Chairman Mao is not.

The singularity of the Holocaust as a public icon of evil is underscored by yet another consideration. Most of the other great horrors of this era are closely tied to Marxism-Leninism. Even after the Revolution of 1989, the public, or at least our intellectual elites, are by no means of one mind about the depredations of Communism. As strange as it may seem, there are still respected apologists who attribute the terrors of Communism to "errors" and "ideological deviations" that distorted the idealistic purposes of the movement. Needless to say, these apologists are seldom to be found among those who lived through the experience of Communism. There are few apologists, however, for National Socialism and the Holocaust.

True, there are occasional "Neo-Nazi" eruptions in the fever swamps surrounding civilized discourse. And there are the historical "revisionists" who claim that the Holocaust never happened. Others say they are only interested in historical accuracy. They want it noted, for instance, that the ovens at Auschwitz could not have been used for the incineration of people, or that there were two million Jewish victims rather than six. One may allow that the standard account of the Holocaust that has assumed mythological proportions is not necessarily accurate in every historical detail. One may not only allow but insist that the Holocaust is so important that historians should indeed pin down every detail, name every name, trace every twist in the day-by-day doing of great evil. Those who are called the Holocaust revisionists, however, are not generally to be found in the company of historians assiduously determined to get at the truth of the matter. Were that their concern, there should be no objection to their efforts. What *moral* difference does it make if not six but three or seven million Jews died in the Holocaust? But the revisionists are typically found in the company of those who seem to have a different argument to make—an argument about the sinister influence of Jews in our society, an argument that is rightly described as anti-Semitic.

Our argument is that, with few exceptions, there is agreement on the evils of National Socialism in a way that there is not agreement, unfortunately, on the evils of Communism. The book of history, so to speak, is closed on Nazism. The telling of its story is culturally embedded, and it is hard to imagine the combination of circumstances that could give rise to that specific evil again. Thus the Holocaust is our culturally available icon of absolute evil. In a society largely indifferent to both the sacred and the demonic, such an icon is precious and fragile. For the sake of our civilization, perhaps for the sake of our souls, the hermeneutics of the Holocaust must be handled with care.

Nonetheless, those who, in many cases for the sake of their souls, rescued the Jews pose problems for many contemporary thinkers. Scholars have a vested interest in one or another way of interpreting human virtue and evil, including the Holocaust. There are those who interpret the Holocaust in terms of the "national character" of the German people, and consequently subscribe to a theory of "collective guilt." That is no doubt a declining school of thought, although it enjoyed a revival with the destruction of the Berlin Wall and the reunification of Germany at the beginning of the last decade of the century. Numerous pundits warned us about the ominous return of the evils associated with "the German character." (Chancellor Helmut Kohl poignantly declared that he had no higher vision for Germany than that it appear "normal," that it "not stick out among the nations of the world.")

The rescuers pose perhaps more formidable problems to the biological and psychological determinists who would subsume and obliterate the category of "the moral" in their explanations of genetic inheritance and social conditioning. Also directly challenged by the research done by the Oliners and others are the students of the "scientific study of morality" such as Jean Piaget and Lawrence Kohlberg. Very directly challenged, too, are Theodor Adorno and his colleagues who, a half century ago, produced *The Authoritarian Personality*. (Interestingly, that study, like *The Altruistic Personality*, was done under the auspices of the American Jewish Committee.) In contrast to much earlier research, the Oliner study is so effective because it is not conducted, first of all, at the level of theoretical argument. Rather, they and their colleagues tell stories, they attend to the day-by-day evidence, and then they try to make sense of what they have discovered. Piaget, Kohlberg, Adorno, and others began with grand explanatory schemes. Explanatory schemes that do not explain the evidence at hand create problems, and we will return to some of those problems.

The Altruistic Personality has now been out several years, but it has not received anything like the attention it deserves. The reviews in prestigious papers and journals were tepidly positive, but few even hinted at the wide-ranging implications of the Oliners' findings. This is a failure, one may say without exaggerating, of historical importance. Given the inexorable toll of time, the sheer fact that the rescuers are rapidly dying off, it is probable that such a study cannot be repeated. The objection has been raised that, even by the mid–1970s, the rescuers were too distant in time from the events of the Third Reich to reconstruct accurately what happened. The objection is not obviated by its being so obvious. There have been other, and more impressionistic, tellings of the story of the rescuers. One thinks in particular of the wondrous book by Philip Hallie, *Lest Innocent Blood be Shed*.[2] It is the story of the French Protestants of Le Chambon-Sur-Lignon, who turned their entire village into a sanctuary and, so to speak, underground railroad for hundreds of Jews during the Nazi occupation. The profiles of quiet heroism in Le Chambon powerfully reinforce the findings in the Oliners' more rigorously scientific study.

The Oliners are keenly aware of the methodological questions that can be raised. They give over almost a hundred and fifty pages simply to explaining and displaying how they went about the study. The evidence of the rescuers was carefully checked and checked again with the evidence of those who knew them and were there at the time. All of this invites a very high level of confidence. In any event, it is almost certainly the best study we are going to get of the subject. To quibble over methodological details (and I have seen no evidence that such quibbles are justified) is to deny ourselves the benefits of a rich and unrepeatable study of the nature of moral character and moral decision making in a world that is critically short of both.

The study focuses on those who were engaged in altruistic actions as determined by clearly measurable criteria. The Oliners write, "We characterize a behavior as altruistic when (1) it is directed towards helping another, (2) it involves a high risk or sacrifice to the actor, (3) it is accompanied by no external reward, and (4) it is voluntary." With striking understatement, the authors add,

"Rescue behavior in the context of the Holocaust meets these criteria." Listing "objective" criteria in this manner may seem excessively "scientific" in the sense of being cold or unfeeling. The Oliners obviously have strong feelings about their subject and, being aware of it, carefully control for it. As a young boy, Samuel Oliner escaped from the Jewish ghetto of Warsaw and was hidden and cared for by Polish peasants who were "Righteous Gentiles." He understandably thinks it only just that the story of such rescuers should be better known.

They should be not only better known but better understood. The deepest motivation of the study is one of intellectual curiosity: Why did ordinary people do such extraordinary things at the risk of their own lives and those of their families? Most of the rescuers in this study did not do extraordinary things just once or twice. Most were engaged in rescue activities over a period of from two to five years. And yet they do indeed seem very ordinary. They are farmers and teachers, entrepreneurs and factory workers, rich and poor, Protestants and Catholics, married and single. They typically insist, all evidence to the contrary, that what they did was not that extraordinary. "I did no more than other people would have done in the same situation" is a constant refrain. Implicit in that statement, one suspects, is the qualifying addition, "other *decent* people." Most of the rescuers do want to believe, despite everything, that other people are basically decent. Many of them make the point that, if other people had known about their necessarily secretive activities, the great majority would have approved of their rescue operations, and maybe even would have joined in.

The Oliners are, no doubt with good reason, not quite so generous in their judgment. They insist that those who actually did engage in rescue activities were notably different, and they doggedly persist in trying to find out why they did what the vast majority of people under the Third Reich did not do. All kinds of possible explanations are entertained and tested. As is the manner in good social science research, variables are controlled, combinations of possibilities are run through the grid of evidence, and at last the researchers come to some conclusions.

Some evidence stands out very clearly. For instance, the difference between the rescuers and the nonrescuers was not class or education or anti-Semitism or philo-Semitism or capacity for leadership or opposition to Nazism or ideological allegiance or myriad other variables that might seem probable. So in what way were these altruistic personalities most significantly different? "What most distinguished them," we are told, "were their connections with others in relationships of commitment and care." They acted virtuously because they belonged to communities of virtue. They did decent, even heroic, things because, in a time of barbarism apparently triumphant, they lived in smaller worlds that were capable of defining decency and disposed to honor heroism. The rescuers were, in the words of the study, "embedded in relationships." They were not, to use the language of Michael Sandel, "unencumbered selves," or, in the language of Lear, "unaccommodated man."

There were three "catalysts" that set most rescuers on their dangerous course. Most were "empathetic," capable of feeling other people's hurt as their own. By far the largest number were "normocentric," centered in communities that had clear and strong beliefs about what we owe our neighbors in need. And a few, a very few, fitted the "autonomous" mode, being people who in an individualistic way understood themselves to be following "universal ethical principles" that dictated their becoming rescuers. In only one instance is an "autonomous" type quoted at length, and she comes across as a very rigid person, a single woman who leaves no doubt about her moral superiority. The worthy things she did notwithstanding, she sounds like a most disagreeable person. One has the impression that she would not be bothered by that observation, since she makes it very clear that she neither needs nor wants the approval of anyone. For the most part, however, the rescuers were empathetic persons embedded in relationships of shared moral norms.

Commentaries on the findings of the Oliners have not noted sufficiently how very antithetical those findings are to the argument of the earlier work, *The Authoritarian Personality*. The findings also challenge very sharply regnant theories in our schools and universities about "moral development" and "values education." Such theories suggest that the course of moral growth is directed toward the maturity of the autonomous moral agent, the unencumbered self. The unencumbered self is liberated from community and convention to choose the rational principles by which he or she will live, allowing a similar freedom for others to live by their chosen rules. The unencumbered self is not capable of self-transcendence, for it is of the essence of being unencumbered that one has transcended everything except the self. Judging by the evidence from the Holocaust, we would be well advised not to expect too much from unencumbered selves when it comes to the moral crunch.

At the same time, it must be recognized that embeddedness in "normocentric" community hardly guarantees that people will do the right thing. On the contrary, those who supported the Nazis and were complicit in the murdering of Jews and others were usually very much embedded in the communal ethos of National Socialism. The Third Reich was acutely aware of the communal nature of moral judgment, and worked hard and skillfully at indoctrinating young and old into its tribal version of moral behavior. One thinks of the brilliantly orchestrated Nuremberg rallies, the *ersatz* religious rites of initiation into the party, and the exhaustively thorough training offered the Hitler Youth. The Nazi leaders were masters of "mass think," and anyone who has watched the propaganda films they produced can only marvel at how difficult it must have been for people, especially young people, to resist the allure of participating in the struggle for the New World that was promised.

Those who did resist heroically, however, were typically not bold individualists who devised their own ethic as a counter against Nazi appeals and pressures. They were countercultural, so to speak, because they were grounded in another culture. They were typically people who were shaped by, and committed to, a communal ethos different from and stronger than the ethos inculcated by the Nazis.

The story of the rescuers offers powerful empirical support for the work of contemporary moral theorists such as Stanley Hauerwas, Alasdair MacIntyre, Gilbert Meilaender, Mary Ann Glendon, and Michael Sandel. These thinkers are, in their various ways, proponents of an ethic of community, character, and virtue. With Aristotle and the main religious traditions of the West, they argue that the moral life consists not in the individual's "choosing his or her own values," but in the learning of virtue by being "embedded in relationships" with those who live virtuously. This is the opposite of the thesis advanced by Adorno and his associates regarding the "authoritarian personality." According to Adorno, the "genuine liberal" is morally mature, which means morally independent. Genuine liberals are people who think for themselves. At the opposite end of the spectrum, according to Adorno, are those who are "ethnocentric" and "inclined toward fascism."

The Adorno thesis continues to hold sway over the thinking of many in our more secularized cultural elites. It is today a commonplace in critiques of the religiously committed, especially fundamentalists and Catholics, who are alleged to be "authoritarian personalities" in thrall to external sources of truth. Such people are, it is said, weak in their need to subordinate themselves to authority that is "heteronomous." They are "fascistic" personalities and were therefore ready prey for Nazism, as well as for any other authoritarian belief system, religious or political, that purports to have a comprehensive explanation of reality. The Adorno scheme relies heavily on psychoanalysis, turning as it does on the resolution of the Oedipus complex and other explanatory devices to which that belief system is prone. The theory of *The Authoritarian Personality* is also, as critics have noted, self-serving to the point of smugness, for the much admired "genuine liberal" turns out to be a creature in the image of the theory's creators.

Adorno and company reached the conclusion that independence is the key to the non-authoritarian personality. Of course their genuine liberal is also courageous and compassionate, although, to be sure, not compulsively or irrationally so. The morally mature know nothing of being bound by the "chain of concern." They are compassionate and courageous *by choice*. One trouble with this approach, however, is that people who fit this description almost never show up among the hundreds of rescuers studied by the Oliners. If it is agreed that rescuing Jews from the Holocaust was a compassionate, courageous, and altogether admirable thing to do, one must ask why so few "genuine liberals" did it. One answer is that, in the real world, there are very few people who fit Adorno's depiction of the genuine liberal. Another answer is that genuine liberals were doing other, and less admirable, things during the Holocaust. Neither answer enhances the attractiveness of the Adorno thesis. In case after case, those whom Adorno's scheme would classify as authoritarian and even fascistic were precisely the people who acted with compassion and courage.

At stake here is more than a dispute over why people did what they did during the Holocaust. At stake is our understanding of the moral life, the sources from which it emerges and the forces that sustain it. In our culture, the Oliners note, "the emphasis on autonomous thought as the only real basis for morality continues to enjoy widespread acceptance." They continue, "The lonely rugged individualist, forsaking home and comfort and charting new paths in pursuit of a personal vision, is our heroic fantasy—perhaps more embraced by men than women but nonetheless a cultural ideal. His spiritual equivalent is the moral hero, arriving at his own conclusions regarding right and wrong after internal struggle, guided primarily by intellect and rationality. It is this vision that underlies much of Western philosophy and psychology." While that heroic fantasy and cultural ideal has a powerful hold on the minds of many, it is almost entirely unrelated to the heroes and heroines of this century's most examined moment of moral truth.

The Oliner findings deserve more attention than they have received not least because they are so pertinent to current public policy disputes. The study provides significant support for those who would redirect policy thinking toward the strengthening of mediating structures, especially the family. Here the "embedded relationships" that produce moral integrity are sustained and transmitted from one generation to another. In our society, of course, almost everybody claims to be "pro-family." But there is a clear division of attitudes toward what is called the "traditional" family. Some "pro-family" advocates treat it as a vestigial and fast-disappearing phenomenon, and propose to put in its place "alternative family structures." Others emphasize the continuing strength, even numerical "normality," of the traditional family, and urge policies that will make it still more viable in the future. On the one side, it is proposed that pro-family legislation on child care and education should be aimed at "socializing" children outside the presumably restrictive confines of "the nuclear family." On the other side, those who are at least as adamant in claiming that they are pro-family oppose such measures as "statist" designs to weaken, if not replace, the traditional role of families.

Similarly with education, the Oliners in their conclusion offer definite recommendations. The study of the moral formation of the rescuers, they urge, makes apparent the importance of schools that transmit clear moral teaching. Current practices in "values education," and especially Kohlberg-type programs of "values clarification," are sharply challenged by an understanding of the experience of the rescuers. As appealing as the Oliners' call for moral education undoubtedly is, it is highly questionable whether the existing public school system can respond adequately. That is because, for the overwhelming majority of Americans, the sources of moral teaching are religious in nature. That is to say, when asked what is the source of morality, nine out of ten Americans respond with an answer that is religious or closely associated with religion. (The Ten Commandments, the Bible, the Sermon on the Mount, the teachings of Jesus, the teachings of the church, and so forth.)

This connection between morality and religion creates great difficulties for those who subscribe to a rigorous reading of "the separation of church and state" in public education. What the Oliners conclude from their study is necessary in education can, it would seem, only be accomplished in a much more flexible educational system— a system that creates adequate space for parental choice, including the choice of schools that make explicit the connection between religion and moral judgment. This is not to suggest that there are not moral traditions, and very moral persons, apart from religion. It is simply that these other moralities are not embraced by the great majority of Americans, which is to say that they are not democratically legitimated. I have made the case elsewhere that biblically rooted moral traditions are essential to providing a secure foundation for a public philosophy that supports a democratic and pluralistic society (see *The Naked Public Square*[3]). It would take us too far afield to elaborate that argument here. There are other questions raised, however, by the treatment of religion in the Oliner study of the rescuers.

The general failure of the churches in Germany—Catholic, Lutheran, and Reformed—to speak out on behalf of the Jews is well known and receives some attention in the Oliner study. It is noted, for example, that many church leaders confined their concern to those Jews who had been baptized, and this the Oliners dismiss as little more than "institutional egoism." In fact, the church situation was considerably more complex than the Oliners suggest, as is elaborated in such authoritative studies as Klaus Scholder's *The Churches and the Third Reich*.[4] In addition, in the hundreds of interviews with rescuers, one cannot help but be struck by the repeated references to the role played by monasteries, convents, and other church agencies. In the context of the Nazi regime's totalitarian ambitions, religion provided almost the only institutional independence— albeit a very limited independence—from the control of the state.

The rescuers make clear that, without religion and the family, there would have been no "social space" for their activities. Their stories are, also in this respect, very similar to the many accounts now available of the struggle to maintain niches of freedom under Communist rule in Eastern Europe. Appreciating the critical role of religion and religious institutions in resistance to the Third Reich, however, cannot obscure the generally dismal record of the churches both in Germany and in the Nazi-occupied territories. It does, however, underscore the pervasively religious nature of resistance to the Nazis, both by the rescuers and by the more politically minded and famous opponents of the regime such as Helmut von Moltke and Dietrich Bonhoeffer. As one rescuer puts it, she and others were trying to do their Christian duty in order to make up for the general failure of the churches to do their duty.

The Altruistic Personality exhibits a certain ambivalence about the religion factor in the story of the rescuers. At one point we are told that 15 percent of the rescuers named religion as a motive for helping Jews. (Of the Jews who were rescued and interviewed in this study, 25 percent say that religion was a primary motive in the activities of the rescuers.) The Oliners observe, "At best, religiosity was only weakly related to rescue." This is an astonishing statement that is at odds with the findings of the study itself. And it is at odds with other statements mandated by the evidence. For instance, the authors discuss at length those rescuers for whom "strong and cohesive family bonds were the primary source of their psychological strength and values." We are told, "Such values were frequently emphasized in a religious context. Both parents inclined toward a strong religious commitment, and rescuers themselves were likely to be characterized by a lifelong religious commitment beginning in childhood."

The findings of the study make it evident that family and religion were the primary and mutually entangled communities of memory and obligation in the lives of the rescuers. Unfortunately, the authors at times attribute motivations to "family" rather than to "religion," when in fact family and religion were usually inseparable. Similarly, the study at points makes the distinction between "ethics" and "morality," on the one hand, and "religion" on the other. But again, the hundreds of interviews suggest that in most cases that is a distinction without a difference. Here is one rescuer speaking about motivation: "My mother was a model of Christian faith and love of neighbor." And another: "My mother taught me to be honest, pray to God, and be respectful to parents and older people—not to tell lies and not to fight in school." And yet another: "My father taught me to work hard and not to tell lies—to be neighborly and polite to elders—to go to church and to be a good Catholic—to be good to your family."

Rescuers repeatedly speak about doing their Christian duty, about the divine command to love the neighbor, and about recognizing Jews as children of the one God. Of course they "learned" these responses in social contexts such as the family, but the present study frequently focuses on the context in which they learned, to the exclusion of the content of what they learned. Typically, the family context and the religious content were one. Moreover, these families did not invent Christian morality on their own. It was transmitted through the preaching, catechesis, and liturgy of the church. Even though church leaders were often supine when it came to public confrontation with the Nazi horror, the effective influence of the church's teaching continued through families and other institutions, producing also the courage and integrity of the rescuers.

Here is Johan, the rescuer quoted at the opening of this chapter: "My grandfather was the most religious man I knew. I had more respect for him than for the minister. He practiced what he preached. He visited the sick; he went to the church to get money for poor people. That's the kind of character he was." It may sound scientific to say that in Johan's case the "grandfather factor" rather than religion was crucial, but that rather misses the point. The content of what Johan learned is at least as important as the question of from whom he learned it. There is certainly no doubt in Johan's mind that his grandfather's motivations were definitively shaped by his understanding of Christian discipleship.

A Dutch rescuer, a man named Dirk, is manifestly impatient with the interviewer's language drawn from social psychology. He protests, "It's not because I have an altruistic personality. It's becaue I am an obedient Christian. I know that is the reason why I did it. I know it. The Lord wants you to do good work. What good is it to say you love your neighbor if you don't help them? There was never any question about it. The Lord wanted us to rescue those people and we did it. We could not let those people go to their doom."

Rescuers typically say that they did not have to think about whether or not to help the Jews. They did not tie themselves in knots trying to "clarify their values." The Oliners write, "To a large extent, then, helping Jews was less a decision made at a critical juncture than a choice prefigured by an established character and way of life." On the basis of the study, however, it is more accurate to say that it was not a choice at all. It was not a matter of choice but of duty. Again and again, rescuers say, "I had no choice." One rescuer observes that she is often asked when she started getting involved in rescuing Jews from the Holocaust. She answers, "We didn't start. It started."

Another says that, if she had not done what she did, "I could never have forgiven myself."

The conclusion is inescapable. These rescuers knew themselves to be bound by the "chain of concern," a chain not forged by their choosing but by an obligation so clear that to deny it would be to deny themselves. Characteristically, it was a question of character. With equal frequency, it was a question of character self-consciously formed by religious faith. It might be argued that there is first a certain kind of personality that then explains itself in terms of the available language of religion. But such an argument overlooks what we know about the relationship between language and reality. Our personalities are shaped by the language—including the "language" of other people's lives—that is available to us. We do not first have an understanding of something, even an understanding of ourselves, and then cast about for the words to express that understanding. The words form our understanding; there is no understanding apart from language. Without words, we cannot think. In other words, we think in words.

In this respect, the Oliner study lacks a certain thoroughness and subtlety in following through on what may be its most valuable finding. The researchers recognize the falsity of the model of the autonomous, rational chooser of ethical rules—of Adorno's "genuine liberal"—but they have not entirely shaken loose from some of the individualistic assumptions underlying that model. Those residual assumptions are most evident in their treatment of communal moral traditions, and religion in particular. We are told, for example, that the altruistic personality is "extensive" rather than "constrictive." The altruistic are people who reach out to people who are not like themselves. They are marked by a "universalistic orientation."

There is a complex, even paradoxical, set of connections here that deserves more careful examination. On the evidence offered by the study—evidence supported by other studies and by everyday experience—people learn "extensivity" within communities that are not all-inclusive, within communities that may even be viewed as "constrictive." It is, as Edmund Burke urged, within the "little platoons" of our lives that concern for the generality is cultivated. The capacity for self-transcendence is sustained only if we have not transcended the communities that form the self.

The splendidly isolated rational decision-maker who has putatively risen above "embedded relationships" is left with nothing but the self. This is one consequence of the radical "turn to the subject" in modern philosophy and ethics. It appears in the form of the "disinterested" and determinedly autonomous individual calculating his or her self-interest, and from that devising a theory for a social contract that will provide security for the self, as well as for other selves engaged in the same calculation. Such a self is a sadly diminished self, abstracted from all the particularities, all the thus-and-sonesses that bestow identity upon the self. Having broken out of the chain of caring, of accountability to others, of community, one is left with nothing more than naked egoism. The data provided by the Oliner study dramatically illustrate the seemingly paradoxical connections between particularity and universality, the extensive and the constrictive. The findings of this research cry out for a much richer interpretation than they have received to date.

There is yet another problem raised in connection with religion and the altruistic personality. The problem is not so much with this study as with the limits of social science. *The Altruistic Personality* has much to say about the role of "normocentric" groups whose values the rescuers "internalized" and whose members reinforced the rescuers in their activities. As we have seen, the most important of such groups are family and religion, the two being usually inseparable. The rescuers testify, however, that these "normocentric" groups were regularly engaged in activities such as prayer and Bible study.

These groups were centered—or *believed* they were centered—in something other than themselves. Social science, by definition, looks at the social group. It can even look at the social group that is looking elsewhere—for instance, a group gathered in prayer. But, *as social science*, it cannot turn from the group to follow the group's look toward the transcendent. And yet, only in this turning from the group, as such, and toward the object of attention by which the group understands itself to be gathered can one enter into the reality of the group. Only then can one understand what the group is about.

Put differently, the "embedded relationships" which this study calls normocentric are not centered in their own norms. They are centered elsewhere. In the language of theologian Wolfhart Pannenberg, they are "exocentric." Social science need not, indeed cannot, say anything about the transcendent reality in which these groups believe they are centered. Social science can and should, however, recognize the importance of the fact that such groups understand themselves to be so centered. The authors cite approvingly the maxim "Situations defined as real are real in their consequences." The implications of that for understanding the rescuers need to be more fully appreciated. The situations defined by many, if not most, of the rescuers is one of exocentricity. They were not autonomous persons "choosing their own values" or discovering rational rules and categorical imperatives that they decided to follow. They define themselves, rather, as persons-in-relationship, as members of communities that taught them to respond to the call of an "other." According to their own testimony, they responded to the "other" who is the Jew because that was expected of them by the "Other," whom they call God.

The exocentricity behind and beyond normocentricity helps us to better understand the altruistic personality. *The Altruistic Personality* advances our thinking about the possibility of self-transcendence. We must examine more thoroughly, however, the claim of the rescuers who are telling us that self-transcendence is not a project of the self, not even of the self in "embedded relationships" with other selves. Self-transcendence, they are saying in various ways, is the consequence of being encountered by the transcendent. Most describe that encounter and the moral response that it entails in the language of religious tradition. Others speak about being encountered by the reality of the way things really are. Thus Johan: "The whole world is a big chain. One little part breaks and it won't work anymore."

However they describe it, the rescuers, who were heroes and heroines in the face of the Holocaust, offer dramatic evidence that self-transcendence is self-surrender to moral truth that we perceive to be not of our own devising. One after another, the rescuers step forward to give their testimony: "I did not choose to do it. I did not start. It started. I had no choice."

6. Discerning
the Community

This chapter is about abortion, and may therefore be an exercise in futility. What that is new can be said about abortion or the debate over abortion? Perhaps very little. But again we are reminded of Dr. Johnson's maxim that we are more in need of being reminded than of being instructed. The prospect of futility is strengthened, however, by the fact that almost everybody has a position on abortion. At least almost everybody who reads books such as this. It is usually a position passionately held. Even those who routinely deplore the "polarization" of the abortion debate are typically part of that polarization. Most of us, I expect, simply wish the issue would go away. But, of course, it will not. It will not so long as there are 40 million abortions per year—1.6 million in the United States alone. And it will not because abortion is inseparably joined to a host of other questions that, far from going away, are pressing upon us with relentless urgency.

Many proposals have been made to reduce the polarization and establish some "middle ground." Mary Ann Glendon of Harvard Law School has significantly advanced our understanding of the abortion debate. In *Abortion and Divorce in Western Law*,[1] she underscores the peculiarity of our American polarization on this question. Other Western countries, less preoccupied with individual rights and more attentive to communal and cultural dynamics, may have something to teach us in avoiding the brutal clash

between "prochoice" and "prolife" factions. Not everybody
who deplores the polarization is so helpful. Glendon's col-
league at Harvard, Laurence Tribe, has addressed the issue
with a book called *Abortion: The Clash of Absolutes*.[2] That
sounds balanced enough, until one reads it and discovers
that it is little more than a legal manual in the war to
maintain the abolition of abortion law effected by the 1973
Supreme Court decision, *Roe v. Wade*. (One review of
Tribe's book was aptly titled, "The Sound of One Absolute
Clapping.")

Proposals for compromise in this debate have not fared
well. Almost everything said on the matter is deemed "controversial." A newspaper account on the former director
of drug policy, William Bennett, said that "he is known
for his controversial views." One of several instances cited
is that "he believes there are too many abortions in the
United States." What, one might ask, is the uncontroversial
position on this question? That there are too few abortions?
That 1.6 million per year is just right? It is a puzzlement.
In the next chapter we will try to puzzle through what
might be done about abortion, especially in the political
arena. The present chapter aims at getting a firmer conceptual grasp on what is at stake in this debate that seldom
achieves the level of genuine debate.

As every high school debater knows, the choice of terms
is a large part of the battle. In this discussion, we will
use the terms prochoice and prolife, well knowing that
this is not agreeable to the several parties in conflict. As
a general rule, it seems only fair to call a position by the
name that its proponents prefer. Prolifers insist that the
opposing position be called "pro-abortion." It is generally acknowledged that prochoicers have an overwhelming
dominance of the prestige media, and there the nomencla-
ture is carefully designed to avoid any suggestion of moral
equivalence in the debate. Most commonly in the major
media, "prochoice" is twinned with "anti-abortion." Many
newspapers and broadcasters describe the conflict in terms

of the "supporters" and "opponents" of "abortion rights," which of course suggests that the prochoice position is positive and the prolife position negative. At the same time, it reinforces the claim that abortion is a constitutional right, which is one of the chief questions in controversy.

In writing a commentary for a major newspaper, I was informed that the paper's policy forbade using prochoice and prolife. Among the permitted formulations was "antiabortion" and "pro-women." The editor proposed, as a "compromise," that I could use prochoice and prolife if the latter was contained within quotation marks. When I rejected that, the paper finally relented and both terms were in quotes. No little victory, that.

The major media know perfectly well what they are doing through these terminological stratagems. One might also argue that they have a perfect right, or at least a legal right, to do what they do. In an era in which opinions are presumably formed by "soundbites," every little word counts. The prolife party, while pathetically outgunned in the media big time, also attends to every little word. When, at the beginning of the 1990s, the Roman Catholic bishops enlisted communications analysts to help get the prolife message across, they discovered that the two most "sacred" words in America's public vocabulary are "choice" and "natural." The resulting message: "Make the natural choice. Choose life."

The battle of sound bites and slogans will continue and, in all likelihood, intensify. The effort to move beyond that battle is viewed with deep suspicion. Many dismiss the effort to elevate the level of public discourse as quixotic, while many more, on all sides of this debate, assume that any such effort is but a camouflage for advancing one position or another. If the author announces that he is prochoice, most readers who identify themselves as prolife will not only skip this chapter and the next but will likely set the book aside for good. Of course the reaction will be the same if I announce that I am prolife. The expedient thing, therefore, is to lament the awful polarization and present oneself as a terribly anguished soul trying with appropriately furrowed brow to think his way through to the middle ground on which all people of good will can agree. The predictable result is either an impossible muddle of the questions engaged by this debate or, more commonly, the sound of one absolute clapping.

And so, reluctantly bidding farewell to some readers, I announce that I am prolife. If they will stay but a minute, I would add that I am convinced that prolife and prochoice proponents have much to discuss. We are going to have to live together in this society for the duration. That consideration should temper our enthusiasm for unholy holy wars that have as their aim the elimination of "the enemy." The purpose of our discussion is not only to achieve agreement, although agreements are certainly to be welcomed. As the late John Courtney Murray was fond of saying, "Disagreement is a great and rare achievement. Most of what we call disagreement is actually confusion." It may well be that, as confusions are clarified, as opponents come to understand one another better, their disagreements and attendant passions will be intensified. That is a risk worth taking. The alternative is to despair of public discourse altogether. That is a risk that democracy—and civilized human beings, for that matter—cannot afford to take.

As we examined earlier, there are good reasons why most of us are averse to labels. We like to think that we think for ourselves, that we are independently minded, even if we are part of what Harold Rosenberg called "the herd of independent minds." If we do acquiesce in accepting a label, we immediately proceed to making clear all the ways in which we are not like other members of the herd. It is so with prochoice, and it is so with prolife. Thus I, too, want to make some distinctions. When I say that I am prolife I am saying that I am more one way than the other—much more.

I am saying that something awful, something ominous, has happened when a society routinely accepts that mothers kill their children. (Yes, I know, there is a great debate over whether the fetus is a child, and we will get to that.) I am also saying that there will always be abortions, probably many abortions, but that we should do our best to encourage alternatives to abortion. Finally, I am saying that, however the abortion controversy turns out, it will not be satisfactory to the more zealous proponents on either side. I am rather certain that it will not be satisfactory to me. In fact, I very much doubt that within the next ten or twenty years it will "turn out" one way or the other in the sense of being determinately settled. But, to the extent that it goes one way or the other, I have no doubt at all about which way I hope it goes.

I first wrote about abortion in 1967. "Abortion: The Dangerous Assumptions" was published in *Commonweal*, the liberal lay Catholic magazine.[3] To my surprise, it won that year's "best article" award from the Catholic Press Association. I had written it, as one writes many things, just to get my mind clear on the subject. *Roe v. Wade* was still six years off, but New York State (along with California and Hawaii) was caught up in powerful agitations for "liberalized" abortion law. Paul Ehrlich's *The Population Bomb*[4] gave vent to a growing anxiety that led to pitting the "quantity of life" against the "quality of life." The quality of life concept I found intuitively disturbing.

That intuition had to do, of course, with my being pastor of a very black and very poor parish in Brooklyn. At St. John the Evangelist we were visited regularly by white, middle-class and upper middle-class people of obvious good will. Some were just slumming, but most really wanted to understand and to help. They were typically appalled by what they saw of the neighborhood, which indeed was in many respects appalling. Frequently someone would say that life in conditions such as these would not be worth living.

I thought a great deal about that. I had read a "quality of life index" by an eminent social scientist at Princeton. No child should be brought into the world, he proposed, unless it is guaranteed a long list of basic securities—physical, psychological, educational, financial. And on the next Sunday I looked into the faces of the hundreds of my people, of God's people, at St. John's and pondered the claim that none of them should ever have been born, for none could begin to qualify by the noted professor's index of a quality life.

Emotional? Irrational? Emotional, to be sure. Irrational, not at all. If children should not be permitted to be brought into the world who do not have a chance at—maybe even a guarantee of—meeting the requirements of such a quality of life index, it rationally follows that the people of St. John's and millions of other Americans should never have been born. Many who espouse the prochoice position shrink from the implications of that proposition. At the same time, it is not unusual to find in Planned Parenthood and kindred literature self-congratulatory calculations of the billions of dollars that abortion has saved our society in welfare, education, and related expenditures. "A child born into a lifetime on welfare will cost us more than half a million dollars," declared a welfare offficial at a government hearing. "Or we can fund an abortion for 150 dollars." He concluded, "It is not the most pleasant reason for abortion, but it is one good reason." So baldly stated, many prochoice advocates might find such reasoning not only unpleasant but abhorrent.

I make no apologies for being powerfully influenced by the discrepancy between my perception of the people of St. John's and the claim that they were living lives not worth living. I would not idealize them, for there is hardly a vice to which humanity is prone that I had not encountered firsthand in Brooklyn. And yet, I was deeply impressed then and am deeply impressed now by the quality of their lives. They are great in their quality of love when it would be so easy to hate; great in their quality of endurance when it would be easy to despair; great in their striving to succeed when they are too readily excused for failing; and especially great in welcoming into lives already heavily burdened the gift of new life. The last mark of greatness has been sadly diminished in the last twenty years. The availability of abortion, and the consequent pressure to abort, has made it easier to "take care of the problem" than to take care of the baby.

It is not the case that the people of St. John's were a drag on society. To be sure, most families were at least partially dependent on welfare for periods of time, but the great majority of adults were hard-working members of the working poor. They performed the jobs that were essential to the survival of the city. Twenty years later, the more radically dependent poor of the underclass are not performing those jobs, and that is one important reason why the city is in grievous decline.

It struck me then that their social betters should have asked the poor what constitutes a life worth living. But, then and now, many who presume to speak for the poor are not on speaking terms with any poor people. It is not surprising that, by the late 1960s, many began to think that the pressure for liberalized abortion law meant that the war against poverty had been replaced by a war against poor people. From time immemorial there have been those who believe that the way to eliminate poverty is to eliminate the poor. In the past, those who held that view did not call themselves liberals. The gravamen of my 1967 article was that the abortion banner was being planted on the wrong side of the liberal-conservative divide. It is an argument that I have continued to make over the years, with only slight evidence of success among those of either prochoice or prolife disposition.

As a people, we are in the unhappy situation of having our constituting rhetoric turned against itself. The many observers who have noted that the American experiment is

unique in being based upon certain moral propositions usually (and rightly) look to Lincoln for the fullest expression
of that constituting rhetoric. That expression, at the same
time quiet and thunderous, is (or used to be) memorized
by every school child. For instance, these words at Gettysburg: "that these dead shall not have died in vain; that this
nation, under God, shall have a new birth of freedom; and
that government of the people, by the people, for the people, shall not perish from the earth." Heady stuff, that. It
represents the linguistic mother lode of the American self-
understanding, of what the deplorably unmusical George
Bush called "the vision thing." Capturing that rhetoric is a
large part of the abortion battle, or any other public contest
of consequence.

Consider the phrase, "a new birth of freedom." Both
prochoice and prolife forces put it in service to their cause.
What could be more obviously a new birth of freedom
than the still new right to choose whether or not to carry
a pregnancy to term? From the other side comes the argument that the idea of pitting liberty against life is alien to
those who believe that every person has an inalienable
right to "life, liberty, and the pursuit of happiness." It
looks like a rhetorical standoff, and sometimes it is just
that. Yet the rhetoric does seem to give the prolife side an
advantage. One reason is that it is *patriotic* rhetoric. Not
all, but a great preponderance of those who are prochoice
also identify themselves as liberals, and current liberalisms
tend to be suspicious of, if not overtly hostile to, the very
idea of patriotism. In this view, the American story is not
dominantly one of success and justice but of failure and
exploitation. In this view, the American experience offers
more reason for repentance than for celebration.

Yet even those who are uneasy about the patriotic telling
of the national story recognize its importance in "winning
the hearts and minds" of the American people. Hermeneu-
tical disputes over the meaning of phrases such as "a new

birth of freedom" become critically important. Six months after Gettysburg, in Baltimore, Lincoln again addressed the question of liberty. "The shepherd drives the wolf from the sheep's throat, for which the sheep thanks the shepherd as his liberator, while the wolf denounces him for the same act. . . . Plainly the sheep and the wolf are not agreed upon a definition of liberty." In the debate over "the abortion liberty" (John Noonan) much of the difference turns on which party is perceived as the sheep and which as the wolf.

The "vision thing" in the telling of the American story has tended to work for the prolife cause. Consider that in 1973 almost every major institution in the country favored the prochoice position. That included the universities, the prestige media, the mainline/oldline churches, and the highest level of the judiciary (as witness *Roe v. Wade*). The one notable exception was the Roman Catholic Church, and those of the American Establishment were not at all sure—as many are not sure now—that the Catholic Church counts as a major institution in this society. It is well to keep in mind that in 1973 the evangelical churches, now so crucial to the prolife effort, did not think abortion such a big moral deal. Certainly abortion was not nearly so important to evangelicals then as school prayer, pornography, and the possibility of a U.S. ambassador to the Vatican. On the eve of *Roe*, the Southern Baptist Convention passed a resolution favoring liberalized abortion.

One may doubt whether ever in American history a major social movement has been able to sustain itself, and even bid fair to prevail, against the almost unanimous opposition of what are taken to be the controlling institutions of society. Yet that is what seems to have happened with the prolife movement. The simple fact that in the 1990s abortion is the most fevered issue in American public life, rivaled only by race, is itself astonishing. The day following the *Roe* decision, the New York *Times* declared that the Court had "settled" the abortion question. To many impartial observers, that would not have seemed an unreasonable judgment at the time.

That things have not turned out that way is not attributable to the sagacity or shrewdness of the prolife leadership. On the contrary, anyone who has followed these battles cannot help but be impressed by the contrast between the near chaos of prolife leadership and the relatively coherent direction of the prochoice cause. Of course there is the myth of the martially organized Roman Catholic Church ordering millions of the faithful to do the bidding of its leaders. Anyone who subscribes to that myth has not been paying close attention over the last three decades. The old line about the Democratic Party now applies here: "I don't belong to an organized religion. I'm a Catholic." Moreover, the church exists to do many things, and not even the most earnest prolifer who is minimally instructed in its teachings would suggest that politicking against abortion should be the Number One activity in the church's understanding of its mission. It is different with organizations such as the National Abortion Rights Action League (NARAL), Planned Parenthood, and National Organization for Women (NOW). They are designed to be single-minded about abortion.

And yet, the religion factor is critically important. In the latter part of the 1970s there was a strong convergence of patriotism, religion, and conservative politics, a convergence that congealed during the Reagan years and shows no signs of dissolving. Social scientist Kristen Luker, herself firmly prochoice, brilliantly analyzed this configuration in *Abortion and the Politics of Motherhood*.[5] While the prochoice party had great advantages in money and access to the media, she noted, the prolifers were much the stronger in grassroots organization, not least of all because of the connection with the churches. In addition, prochoice women tend to be career minded. They can give money and use the influence of their positions, but they have little time for the cause. Prolife activists, on the other hand, are overwhelmingly composed of women who organize from their homes, making phone calls, helping to get out mailings, and doing the myriad other things necessary to keep a grassroots movement moving. Faye D. Ginsburg has more recently reinforced Luker's findings on the importance of class, education, and career choice in giving the prolife cause an organizational advantage among women.[6]

Those factors, plus the patriotism-religion-conservatism connection, powerfully drive the prolife effort. In addition, there are numerous liberals who are also prolife, and some conservatives, notably of the libertarian variety, who are emphatically prochoice. The "country club" Republicanism that was so dominant prior to the Reagan era is generally conservative in a distinctly prochoice way. There are relatively small organizations such as Feminists for Life, but they clearly understand themselves to be cutting across the ideological grain, and their feminism is much too tame for the more radical feminists who tend to rule the prochoice organizations.

It has been said that America is so large and various that almost any generalization about it can be supported by impressive evidence. That is doubly true of political and ideological constellations in America. Yet, with respect to the profiles of the prochoice and prolife movements, the work of Luker, Ginsburg, and others is persuasive. The profiles seem to be working out in terms of political alignments. It is fair to say today that no Democratic politician with national ambitions can be identified as prolife. It is not quite so clear that a Republican presidential candidate could not be prochoice, although it would almost certainly be a severe handicap, running the very high risk of a third party challenge. Underlying these political divisions are deeper cultural and moral fissures.

Robin Toner, writing for the New York *Times*, has covered both prolife and prochoice rallies over the years. She is struck that these demonstrations bring together "two different Americas, two different cultures." The difference, she says, is dramatically evident in the dominant vocabularies employed. Prochoice rallies are dominated by the language of "rights and laws," prolife rallies by the language of "rights and wrongs." It is, I believe, an astute perception that helps us understand the nature of a crisis in which two "cultural-linguistic communities," two fundamentally different perceptions of reality, are in conflict. It is by no means evident that our polity and habits of public discourse can succeed in bringing these vocabularies into a semblance of civil debate. The alternative to civil debate may be civil war.

Societies can, just conceivably, sustain a language of rights and wrongs without a language of rights and laws. It is highly doubtful that a language of rights and laws can be sustained without a language of rights and wrongs. If the appeal to rights and laws is perceived to be against strongly held convictions about rights and wrongs, those rights and laws will be viewed as lacking moral legitimacy. Although the explicit language of morality comes more naturally to one side than the other in the abortion debate, both sides are making unmistakably moral arguments. Both sides accuse their opponents of being concerned about more than abortion, claiming that they have a hidden agenda. At the same time, both sides insist that the abortion debate is about much more than abortion. Both sides are right.

Prolifers say that their concern is to prevent the killing of innocent human beings. Now, *if* one believes that four thousand abortions per day means that four thousand innocent human beings are being killed each day in America, that would seem to be concern enough. *If* one believes that, it is difficult to imagine what other issue in American public life could rival abortion in its moral urgency. At the same time, prolifers frequently say that the abortion debate is about more than abortion. They insist that it is about euthanasia, the legal protection of the severely handicapped, genetic engineering, and other questions of ominous importance.

Those in the prochoice camp also say that prolifers are concerned about more than abortion. When they say that, however, they mean that prolifers are *really* motivated by a desire to undo the new freedoms of women, to reestablish the traditional family as normative, and to force sexual activity back into the confines of marriage. Too often, prolife advocates deny the charge. The denial is understandable on the level of political forensics, but it is probably a mistake. Pregnancy and abortion are, after all, connected with sexuality, and sexuality with institutions of family, marriage, and parenthood. When it uncouples abortion from these other questions, the prolife cause inadvertently plays into the hand of its opposition. The moral, cultural, and legal uncoupling of sexual behavior from its consequences and communal contexts is at the heart of the "new freedom" that is so radically in need of maintaining the logic and law of *Roe v. Wade.*

It would in some ways be easier were the conflict simply between the party of "rights and laws" and the party of "rights and wrongs." In that case it is likely that the party of rights and wrongs would finally prevail in a democratic society, for rights and laws cannot be sustained in the face of a majority perception that they are based upon a terrible wrong. In reality, the prochoice party, the party of rights and laws, is also a party of rights and wrongs. That is to say, while many of them are uncomfortable with the explicit language of morality (in part because of its religious associations in American culture), prochoice advocates generally believe that theirs is the moral position.

While some demand only autonomy and the right of women to do whatever they want, the prochoice argument is typically an argument for *justice*, an inescapably moral category. The prochoice movement is greatly handicapped by its inability, so far, to make moral arguments in public. By persistently accusing its opponents of wanting to "impose their morality" on the society, the prochoice movement reinforces the popular impression that their

opponents are the party of morality. Americans are incorrigible in wanting to believe that they are a moral people. All
the money and all the media access in the world will not
likely prevail, in the near term or long term, against those
who are in possession of what George Bush so witlessly
called "the vision thing."

This is the reality examined by Daniel Callahan in "An
Ethical Challenge to Prochoice Advocates."[7] Callahan, a
former Catholic and director of the Hastings Center in New
York, is no enemy of the prochoice movement. On the
contrary, in 1970 he published a large and immensely influential book, *Abortion: Law, Choice and Morality*.[8] Written
under the auspices of the Alan Guttmacher Institute, a prochoice think tank, Callahan's *Abortion* quickly became an
authoritative text invoked by courts, pundits, and activists
who favored liberalizing or abolishing abortion law. Two
decades later, Callahan writes, "I have not changed my
view on the legal issue in any significant way."

But Callahan believes he was misunderstood. While he
urged that abortion is a private choice and should be left
up to the woman, he also insisted that "it is still a serious
moral choice" that is worthy of public no less than private
reflection. Years later, he ruefully writes, "I could not have
been more naive, more hopelessly optimistic, in thinking
that such reflection would be acceptable. The prochoice
movement has in fact never known quite what to do with
the moral issue." The leaders of the movement have by
default ceded morality to the opposition. Many prochoice
advocates have concluded that "to concede that [abortion]
is a *serious* moral choice and to have a public discussion about that choice is politically hazardous, the opening
wedge of a discussion that could easily lead once again to
a restriction of a woman's right to an abortion." "Better,"
they think, "to declare the whole topic of the morality of
abortion off limits."

Callahan cites the familiar data indicating that most
Americans are morally uneasy about abortion. Minimally,

they think some reason, some good reason, must be given to justify abortion. "The prolife movement has effectively capitalized on this uncertainty," Callahan writes, "appealing to the moral uneasiness of many and bringing to the surface qualms and doubts shunted aside by the prochoice movement." For some people, choice itself is the beginning and end of morality; for most people it is just the beginning, depending on whether the choice is right or wrong. According to Callahan, the question of morality "does not end until a supportable, justifiable choice has been made, one that can be judged right or wrong by the individual herself based on some reasonably serious, not patently self-interested, way of thinking about ethics." The failure to articulate such a standard, says Callahan, not only puts the prochoice movement in political jeopardy but "is a basic threat to moral honesty and integrity."

In the late 1960s, leading up to *Roe*, the basic arguments for legalized abortion were crafted and effectively disseminated. The arguments, according to Callahan, were these: illegal abortions are killing and maiming many thousands of women; women need a backup to ineffective contraception, although contraception should remain the primary means of birth control; the allegedly large number of unwanted pregnancies should be reduced—only wanted children should be born; while the abortion decision is morally and psychologically difficult, it is a woman's to make; while abortion should be legally available and financially affordable, efforts should be made to change the economic and domestic conditions that force women into unwanted pregnancies.

That was twenty years ago. Since then, says Callahan, there have been major changes—political, scientific, and ideological. The most obvious political change is the emergence of a strong prolife movement. "While this movement has often been stereotyped by its opponents as nothing but religious conservatism, that is hardly accurate," he writes. Among liberals gravitating to the prolife movement, says

Callahan, are many women who are feminists. "They see in abortion a resort to violence similar to that used for centuries by men against women: the use of power by the strong against the weak, both the physical power of violence and the cultural power to define the unwanted out of the human community altogether." But the prolife movement has found "its greatest strength" by focusing on the issue that the prochoicers find "most discomforting and awkward," namely, "the moral status of the fetus."

The awkwardness is reinforced by scientific advances in fetal health, and the lowering age of fetal viability, now down to less than twenty-four weeks. The sonogram allows women and, through photography appearing in magazines such as *Life*, the general public to see the fetus *in utero*. "Taken together," says Callahan, "these scientific developments have brought the fetus more squarely before the public eye." The prolife movement has not failed to capitalize on this change. The most striking ideological change, on the other hand, has been brought about by the emergence of prochoice leaders who have forgotten or suppressed the original arguments for legalized abortion. "They have shifted the emphasis almost entirely to a woman's right to an abortion, whatever her reasons and whatever the consequences," Callahan writes. Much less is heard about abortion as a tragic moral choice, and almost nothing about the need to reduce the number of abortions. "No number of abortions seems to be too many."

Callahan believes that the prochoice movement has become the mirror-image of its opponents. "If the prolife movement exclusively stresses the rights of the fetus, then the prochoice movement must exclusively stress the rights of women. If the prolife movement says that abortion is oppressive and murderous, the prochoice movement must then say it is liberating and morally unimportant. If the prolife movement says that every abortion choice is wrong, whatever the reason, then the prochoice leadership implies that every choice is right, whatever the choice."

This, according to Callahan, is a dramatic change from the more "measured and careful" prochoice leadership of two decades ago. The main reason for the change is the success of the prolife movement, joined to the media's predilection for polarized positions. The result is that the prochoice leadership is losing its ability to speak to the 60 percent of the American public that falls in a "zone of ambivalence and nuance" with respect to the reasons that justify abortion. The prochoice leadership is averse to such distinctions and, when pressed on the moral issues, "usually reacts with anger, confusion, or denial." In sum, "It does not know what else to do with them."

We cannot treat here the entirety of Callahan's long and complex argument, but it offers a valuable peek into the anxieties of those who embrace the prochoice position, and it has everything to do with the next chapter's discussion of how the great abortion wars may turn out. In making its case, says Callahan, the prochoice movement is relying on arguments that are either "false or highly misleading." The first argument is that abortion restrictions represent a war of men against women, with men intent upon keeping women in reproductive thralldom. The second is that abortion is not a primary means of birth control but a backup to contraceptive failure. The third is that abortion reduces the dependence of women upon men, giving them full control over their reproduction. Fourth, it is said that, given the freedom of choice, women will make free choices. Fifth, it is asserted that it does not matter what choice women make so long as it is their own choice.

In exposing these "false or highly misleading" propositions, Callahan draws on information familiar to students of the subject but seldom aired in public. Far from prochoice vs. prolife being a war of men against women, women are significantly more prolife than men. In response to the second proposition, at least 40 percent of all abortions are now repeat abortions. Abortion has become for many the primary means of birth control, just as it is for millions of women in Eastern Europe. As to the claim that the easy availability of abortion increases the woman's freedom to choice, studies show that it is men who have been newly empowered. Callahan cites a Guttmacher study showing that 30 percent of women who have abortions have them because someone else, not the woman, wants it. Other studies suggest that more than 90 percent of women say they had no choice, often citing pressures from boyfriends and husbands. Finally, Callahan rebuts the claim that it does not matter what choice women make so long as it is their own choice. "That," he writes, "is a hard position to sustain. . . when the choice is to abort a female fetus simply because it is female; or to have an abortion to please (or spite) a husband or boyfriend; or to have repeat abortions because of a casual attitude toward the use of contraceptives; or to conceive fetuses for experimental purposes or commercial profit."

By promulgating falsehoods and by evading the need for moral reflection, Callahan fears that the prochoice movement is, however inadvertently, demeaning women. He repeatedly says the movement runs great "risks" in honestly confronting the moral questions, but it will continue to lose its credibility if it does not. "A prochoice position that would make the value of early human life depend solely upon private choice and the individual exercise of power. . . fails to understand the importance of communal safeguards against capricious power over life and death." Callahan says that nothing has so baffled him over the years as "the faintly patronizing, paternalistic way in which, in the name of choice, it has been thought necessary to protect women from serious moral struggle."

Risking moral argument, the prochoice cause must also risk some political compromises. Callahan's proposed compromises are small but substantive. Real choice in matters of serious moral consequence requires reflection and psychological freedom, and he therefore thinks the movement should not object to a mandatory waiting period of a few days. "A flat rejection of that possibility," he says, "suggests a desire to maximize abortion rather than to increase choice." There are other "compromises." Late abortions would be sharply restricted, parents of teenagers would be notified, federal funding of abortion would be available only for medical or clear health reasons, mandatory counseling and waiting periods would be in place, and there would be serious efforts to reduce the number of abortions, especially of repeat abortions. Needless to say, all these measures are relentlessly opposed by prochoice leaders today, and there is no indication that they will be swayed by the argument of Daniel Callahan, despite his historic contributions to the prochoice cause.

Callahan sums up his argument in a manner that may at first seem even-handed. "The great weakness of the prolife movement is that it has not been willing to trust individuals with free and private moral choice. The prochoice movement has fallen into a different trap. It has been unwilling to trust the moral issues to public debate." In fact, however, the prochoice leadership may see something that Callahan's argument misses. To engage the "moral issues" in public is to publicly acknowledge that those issues, by definition, cannot be left to "free and private choice." If they are legitimate issues for public deliberation, it is assumed that they are legitimate issues for public decision. The most obvious and chief issue, of course, is the status of the unborn.

However it outraged many Americans, Ronald Reagan as president was undoubtedly effective when he repeatedly said, "I can't get over the simple fact that there are two lives involved in the abortion decision." That from the beginning of pregnancy there is life in the womb is beyond reasonable dispute. That it is human life is similarly indisputable. By asserting criteria for "fully human life," one can argue that the fetus is only potentially a human being. But then, depending upon the criteria chosen, we are all only potentially the fullness of humanity that we may attain. It would seem to be incontrovertible that nothing that does not have the potential of becoming a human being is a human being, and nothing that has the potential of becoming a human being is not a human being.

The question in the abortion debate, I suggest, is defining the human community for which we accept public responsibility. The problem then becomes how to exclude some forms of human life, e.g., the fetus, without by the same criteria excluding others whom we do not want to exclude. Tests such as "viability" become utterly useless at this point, for it is obvious that a baby two weeks after birth is not viable in the sense that it can live on its own. In addition there are the many thousands of "vegetables" and "near-vegetables" in hospitals and nursing homes across the country, all of whose lives are not "viable." Not for nothing, one may conclude, has the prochoice leadership been, in Callahan's words, "unwilling to trust the moral issues to public debate."

As we will see in the next chapter, the public debate—and its political repercussions—turns very much on a moral discernment that puts the prochoice cause at a severe disadvantage. This becomes more evident when the question is not "When does life begin?" but "When do *we* decide that a human life has moral and legal status?" Robin Toner's divide between the "two Americas" is thrown into sharp relief when, for example, the question turns to infanticide. Some who favor unlimited abortion rights have candidly proposed that there be a "trial period" of a week or two after a baby is born. Only after birth, they say, can a really thorough examination for defects be conducted, and it should be permissible then to "terminate" those children who are severely defective.

Almost all Americans, one expects, think that infanticide is a public, not a private, question. Those who support the logic and law of *Roe v. Wade*, however, are hard put to explain why they oppose infanticide without publicly raising the suspicion that *any* line drawn for the legal protection of an infant is entirely arbitrary. Here the cultural and moral conflict between the two Americas is brought to a head. It is a conflict between those who believe that human beings possess "unalienable rights" that we are bound to respect and those who, in various ways, argue that rights in law and life are "fictions" that we can more or less make up as we go along. Needless to say, the weight of the American national story, reinforced by biblical religion, is overwhelmingly supportive of the first position.

Leaving it at that, however, may give the misleading impression that there is an unbridgeable chasm between the two Americas. One must at least want to believe that that impression is misleading. Daniel Callahan's wan hope for a prochoice leadership that would publicly engage the great moral questions is not misplaced. If we as a people are incapable of a semblance of civil discourse about the kind of society we intend to be, the democratic experiment, and all of us along with it, will be greatly diminished.

Nowhere today is the battle line between the two Americas drawn so sharply as over the issue of abortion. We have noted that the abortion conflict is about ever so much more than abortion. It is about human sexuality, marriage, family, parenthood, and the "taboos" that have been thought necessary to civilized existence. It is also about euthanasia, "assisted suicide," genetic engineering, the farming and harvesting of fetuses for medical experimentation, and related developments. With respect to the latter group of issues—the "medical breakthroughs" that some insist are more accurately understood as cultural breakdowns—the prolife party is frequently depicted as being alarmist. Prochoice advocates, on the other hand, are depicted as being mindlessly insouciant about the implications of changes uncritically embraced. There is considerable truth in both depictions. One runs the risk of sounding quixotic in expressing the hope that the present polarization between prolife and prochoice will not entirely preclude the possibility of civil conversation about some of the other ominous developments that are now upon us.

We need not speculate about what *may* be down "the slippery slope" on which we find ourselves. The truly ominous changes are the stuff of our daily newspapers. These things are happening now. Consider the much discussed case of Nancy Cruzan. On December 15, 1990, the feeding tube was removed, and some expected that she would die in time for Christmas. The statements from the Hemlock Society and sundry "death with dignity" lobbies made clear that they were in a celebrative mood. They claimed a great victory. But many Americans, and not only those who call themselves prolife, wondered.

The Cruzan case had been to the Supreme Court and back. Every mindless talk show in the country had at least once chatted up the pros and cons of "letting Nancy die." For eight years, following an automobile accident, Miss Cruzan had been given food and fluid through a tube. She was said to be, in the current jargon, in a persistent vegetative state (PVS). An obviously caring family had long insisted that "It is time to let Nancy go." She was not dead by any current medical measure. She was not "brain dead," nor had the vital signs ceased. After the tube was removed, ten days later, she was finally pronounced dead, and there were sighs of relief.

Those who had taken care of Nancy Cruzan over the years had a different reaction to the removing of the tube. Nurse Sharon Orr said, "The Humane Society won't let you starve your dog. They don't starve death row inmates." Another nurse said it would have been easier to handle the situation if Miss Cruzan had been killed with a lethal injection. "I'm not saying that that's a good option," she added, "but it would be more humane than the suffering she'll have to go through." Nurse Orr protested the claim that Miss Cruzan was in a vegetative state. "Do carrots cry? Nancy has tears." Another nurse, Debbie Schnake: "We had Nancy long enough that she's almost like a member of our family." She tearfully described a relationship of "day-in, day-out touching and loving given daily here by every shift."

Dr. Donald Lamkinds, the director of the Missouri medical center where Nancy died, observed, "There's two kinds of law here: our legal laws—those are society's laws—and moral law. Moral law is God's law; it comes from religion. Man's laws said it's all right, but that doesn't change the moral law." Dr. James Davis, the one who actually withdrew the tube, acknowledged that the hospital staff was hurt and angry, feeling that all their caring of Miss Cruzan over the years had been judged senseless and misguided. Davis said he was sure he had done the right thing, but he was not sleeping well at nights. "I had a dream last night that I went back into her room and she was sitting up, talking to her mother," he said. He added, "But that turns out to be a nightmare."

Who won and who lost in the Cruzan case? Was it a civilized step toward "death with dignity," or a brutal turn, cloaked in the rhetoric of compassion, toward ridding ourselves of the burdensome among us? Certainly it was a radical turn from long-established moral principle. The official directive for Catholic health facilities declares: "The directly intended termination of any patient's life, even at his own request, is always morally wrong." There is nothing peculiarly Catholic in that claim. In Western medicine, that principle has been in place since Hippocrates in the fifth century B.C. It has often been violated, also in modern times—massively so under Nazism and Communism—but civilized people have adhered to it in principle. No longer. What the Missouri court ordered and what Dr. Davis did was directly intended to terminate the life of Nancy Cruzan. There is also no blinking the fact that they intended to kill her by starvation and dehydration.

We are told that death by starvation is particularly ugly. Even with heavy sedation, the body goes into terrible spasms and the face becomes grotesquely disfigured. It takes a long time to starve to death. As the nurse said, why not something quick, like a lethal injection? Once we have directly intended to terminate a life, there would be no moral difference in doing it neatly and, presumably, painlessly. There would be this difference: we could not conceal from ourselves what we are doing. There could be no more talk about letting people die. With lethal injections, it would be obvious that we are in the business of killing people. By starving Nancy Cruzan to death, we are in the killing business already. We can debate whether we are right or wrong in doing this. We can go around the track once more on all the arguments about "right to life" and "right to death." But nobody should deny that we are, in fact, killing people.

The stark realities are obfuscated, sometimes deliberately, by much talk about "prolonging death" by the imposition of new medical technologies. Nancy Cruzan was not dying, except in the sense that all of us are daily closer to death. It was unanimously acknowledged that she might have lived another ten years or more. Nor was she heavily burdened with medical technology. Surrounded by caring nurses, she received food and fluid through a tube. It was "artificial," to be sure, but far from an "extraordinary" or "high technology" treatment. It is "artificial" to provide food to a helpless person by lifting a spoon to his mouth. That is not the "normal" way human beings receive sustenance. But the drift today, encouraged by ever so permissive "medical ethicists," is to erase the distinction between ordinary and extraordinary means. Any care, including the provision of food and fluid, is deemed an extraordinary means. At least in cases where it is judged that a life is not worth living.

It is noted that Miss Cruzan might have lived another ten years or more. "Lived?" comes back the incredulous response. "What kind of life would that be? And how cruel to impose the burden of that lingering 'existence' upon her loving family!" One can understand the concern and compassion in that response. But now we are into the thick of the matter. Adopt a "quality of life" index by which some lives are determined to be not worth living, and join that to the permission to directly intend to kill. Agree, further, that starving people to death is clumsy, unseemly, and cruel. With those pieces in place, are we not now ready to take our hypodermic needles and lethal doses and get serious about the killing business?

At the risk of entering upon a heavily mined field, we must ask whether we can speak about lives not worth living without remembering the phrase, *lebensunwertes Leben*? It means in German, lives unworthy of life. It was used by the Nazis to justify the directly intended killing of the burdensome. Yes, I know that none of us are Nazis, and this is not Germany in the 1930s. This is America, and we are motivated by kindness and compassion. It cannot happen here. *We* would never do that kind of thing. But leave motivations and our putatively superior virtue aside for a moment. What if, just what *if*, we are, in fact, doing not only that kind of thing but that very thing? The question is not intentions. The question is the thing itself.

In hospital wards and nursing homes across the country, there are thousands upon thousands of patients who are, by the criteria applied to Nancy Cruzan, *lebensunwertes Leben*. They are, as her undoubtedly loving family said of her, "already dead." We are not really killing them, we tell ourselves. We are simply helping them to be what they already are—dead. But, it is objected, witnesses testified that she herself would not want to live under the circumstances of these last eight years. Perhaps so, although the court testimony was indecisive. As a vibrant young woman in her twenties, we can well imagine her saying, "If I was ever in a situation where I couldn't do anything for myself and was a great burden to others, I wouldn't want to go on living." Such a person might even have gone on to say, "If I am ever in that situation, I hope somebody will kill me."

There is no evidence that Nancy Cruzan said those things, but she *might* have. The Supreme Court decision in the Cruzan case indicated that there is a right to refuse medical treatment (food and fluid presumably being defined as "medical treatment"). The current state of law and "medical ethics" is redefining "choice" to include choices made for us by others. "Substitute judgments" and "surrogate judgments" by the family will be enough. Those who "know the patient best" can determine that *they* would not want to live under such circumstances, and therefore it is legally determined that he or she does not want to live. More precisely, it is determined by substituted judgment that he or she has chosen to be killed.

The older ethic did not forbid the withdrawal of feeding tubes under every circumstance. The tube could be removed when death was imminent, or when it was counterindicated, i.e., when it exacerbated an existing condition or created seriously threatening side effects. What was forbidden is the direct intention to kill. What was forbidden is what was done to Nancy Cruzan and will now, almost certainly, be done to many others. In the past, there were grey areas; that was understood. It was understood that civilization rests in large part upon ambiguities. But now we have it in lethal black and white. License has been given to kill those whom the living consider to be no better than dead.

In response to Nancy Cruzan's death, the two Americas (recall "rights and laws vs. rights and wrongs") found expression in two prestigious editorial voices.[9] The lead editorial in the *New York Times* was titled, "The Achievement of Nancy Cruzan." The point was that her being allowed to die "with dignity" was her contribution to a more rational approach to death and dying. Albeit expressed in a thoroughly secularized manner, the suggestion was that her death was redemptive. Her suffering and death were not pointless; she has made it possible for other people to end their suffering by death. "I am damn proud of her," said Nancy Cruzan's father. The *Times* warmly agreed that he should be.

The editorial message of the *Wall Street Journal* was elegiac rather than celebrative. Acknowledging that the plight of the hopelessly ill "raises difficult questions of morality and conscience," the editors were uneasy. There was a time when grey areas of ambiguity were respected, when questions about treatment or non-treatment "would be resolved by a family, its doctor and its clergyman." "However the matter was resolved, life would go on for that family, as it would for other families as they passed through these periods of seemingly unbearable distress. But no more."

Among the many troubling aspects of the Cruzan case is precisely that it was so publicized, and the suffering of the family so exploited in order to advance a political and legal change. "In America now," the *Journal* observes, "Nothing is allowed to be merely personal. Instead, it is a matter of 'policy' that simply must be 'debated' at great length in public, no matter how grotesque or obscene the spectacle of conducting such business around the bent form of a woman in a vegetative state." People have little tolerance for areas where discretion, prudence, and conscience rule. "What they want is a *law* or a *judgment*. They want a judge to use his authority to posit a *right*, and 'settle' the debate." When the Cruzan case came before the Supreme Court, Justice Scalia warned that the Court "will destroy itself" if it continues to take up controversies wherever human irrationality and oppression may theoretically occur. The editors offer this corollary: "This society will damage its civil cohesion if it insists on making judges arbiters of disputes that should be matters mainly of morality mediated by conscience." That there are not social institutions that are trusted to be guides for conscientious action is, in the editor's view, largely the result of the default of the churches and other agencies of religion.

"[Religious leaders] essentially decided during the past 20 years that people could fend for themselves on matters of personal morality while the churches joined the 'struggle' to establish social 'rights' whose imprimatur comes

from the courts, America's unique bishopric." More than
three centuries ago, when dealing with death was more
a part of everyday life, John Donne asked: "What is so
intricate, so entangling as death? Who ever got out of a
winding sheet?" The *Journal* concludes: "Nancy Cruzan,
entangled eight years in publicity, is now in peace. As a
society we somehow have to rediscover what we already
know as individuals and families—that death's intricacies
are beyond the grasp of codes or judges."

It certainly does not hold for all the differences of editorial bias between the *Times* and the *Journal*, but, in
this instance, the former is the voice of rights and laws,
the latter of rights and wrongs. I have not quoted the
Times editorial at length because the viewpoint is so familiar, clearly dominating the media. The *Journal*'s is the
countercultural viewpoint—that there are some things on
which we should not have clear "policy," that there are
some issues that simply cannot be "settled" by law. Expanding on that viewpoint, one might argue that there are
many dimensions of life that simply do not lend themselves
to policies or court decisions. In these spheres we must
rely upon culture and morality—upon principles being in
place, and upon habits and institutions that nurture the
conscientious observance of such principles. In short, we
must rely upon virtues. The objection is raised that, in the
absence of virtues, we must rely upon policies and court
orders. But what if reliance on policies and court orders
actively undermines virtue? What if, as I believe is true in
the present case, policies and court orders invite the doing
of that which virtue would inhibit, even if it cannot always
effectively prohibit?

To speak, as we have, of our being in the killing business
will strike some readers as altogether too harsh. We are in
the business of alleviating suffering, of permitting people
to die with dignity. Such are the euphemisms by which we
disguise the deed. The old expression "mercy killing" had
the merit of appealing to good intention (mercy) while

candidly denoting the deed (killing). In the long, complex history of our civilization's pondering questions of life and death, the law and moral sentiment allowed killing in three circumstances: self defense or defending another, the waging of a just war, and the retributive justice of capital punishment in the instance of murder.

Now, so suddenly, we are opening up a vast new sphere of license. Note that the three established exceptions against killing did not involve innocent lives. The combatant in war, unlike the noncombatant, and the deadly attacker are not considered to be innocents, and those executed are first found guilty of murder. The "vegetables" in our hospitals and nursing homes are guilty of nothing. They are simply in a very bad way not of their choosing. But the thought insinuates itself that they are "guilty" of being a burden to others. It is passing strange that the same people who describe ours as a society driven by selfishness and greed are, at the same time, so insouciant about giving people permission to kill others whom they find burdensome. When it comes to terminating the lives of others, the selfish and greedy will presumably act in selfless devotion to the well-being of others.

Underlying this shift is also an obsession with youth and health that doesn't know what to do with suffering other than to get rid of it. Suffering and fragility that we cannot "fix" is an affront to our need to be in control. There was once respect for suffering nobly borne, or at least respect for the idea. Biblical spirituality inculcated the idea of suffering as redemptive, and invited a response of altruistic caring from others. Such patterns of thought are now utterly alien to the dominant attitudes in our society, including the attitudes of the great majority who profess to be believing Christians and Jews. The idea of redemptive suffering, if indeed it is ever raised, is dismissed as "romantic," even a rationalization for cruelty.

There is nothing worse than suffering, it is now believed. Suffering is a surd, a meaningless and threatening intrusion upon the way we choose to order our lives. The only rational response to it is to eliminate it. Far from being romantic, the older attitude toward suffering was relentlessly realistic, recognizing that each of us is radically dependent upon a conspiracy of caring to shelter one another in time of direst need. Now we call it kindness to put them out of their misery, denying even to ourselves that the misery we cannot bear is the burden that they are to us. The "us" is the living, the healthy, the strong, who want to get on with our lives, who want to live our lives as *we* want to live our lives before our time comes to die. Maybe, we say in our innermost heart, science will come up with the answers that will delay death indefinitely. What we tell ourselves is a more rational and humane approach to suffering is, as Ernest Becker tried to teach us, driven by "the denial of death." Half suspecting that that is the case, people throw themselves more desperately into their private little immortality projects. Unable to bear the reality of death, we refuse to bear with the dying.

It is not likely that the "angels of death" will anytime soon spread out through our hospitals and nursing homes to go about their "mission of mercy" on a systematic and massive scale. For one thing, there are too many nurses like Sharon Orr and Debbie Schnake who persist in believing that their patients are persons. For another, doctors do not want the idea to get around that when they come to visit one cannot be sure whether they come to care or to kill. Not systematically and massively but selectively patients will be killed. Patients who have loving families will be first. Nancy Cruzan would be alive today were it not for her family whose love made her such an emotional "burden" to them. If they had not cared so much, she would not have been killed. She was, as it were, killed by love.

There are many thousands of Americans who love grandma or grandpa or their elderly wives or husbands too much to allow them to go on lingering in their pitiful state. Now that directly intended killing is permitted, a way can be found to do the merciful deed. At present, a court order is required. But judges are compassionate. And, if it is done in the absence of a court, ours is a forgiving society, especially since it has now been determined that there is no wrong to forgive.

In this chapter, then, we have touched on some of the reasons why the abortion debate is about ever so much more than abortion. It may not be possible, but we must surely try, as a society, to address these other questions in a way that is not predetermined by the abortion conflict. I say it may not be possible because, on both the prochoice and the prolife sides, the argument is made that these "other" questions are not really other. They are, it is said, simply extensions of the conflicting moral logics that drive the abortion debate. Unfortunately, that may be true. It may be that the hope for a genuinely civil moral discourse is wishful thinking, that the future promises no more than an interminable warfare in the public arena. In the next chapter, we will look at how these questions are presently working their way through our intimidatingly complex political system.

7. Defending
the Community

In 1989 the Supreme Court's decision in *Webster* suggested that the abortion debate will be returned to the democratic process. Columnist George Will is among the many who recognize that the Court had in the past made an awful mess of the abortion question. He derides the incoherence and "anti-constitutional nonreasoning" of the Court's abortion rulings. He also recognizes that the abortion debate is not really over the question of when human life begins. "The indisputable fact," he observes, "is that a fetus is alive and biologically human. . . . Biology does not allow the abortion argument to be about when human life begins. The argument is about *the moral significance and hence the proper legal status of life in its early stages*."[1]

Will then reflected on what this means for our politics. He was skeptical of George Bush's prolife position (no abortions except in cases of rape, incest, and direct threat to the mother's life). But he says that the president is stuck with it, as are many other politicians who have declared themselves on the prolife side. Will assumes that the prolife position is a political albatross. He writes, "Many millions of voters who would recoil from enactment of the abortion policy embraced by Bush and the GOP platform vote Republican anyway because . . . abortion has been largely a subject of litigation rather than legislation." But, Will says, if *Roe v. Wade* is reversed, the abortion issue will be brought to "an instant boil" in fifty state legislatures, and then the

Republicans, if they stick with the prolife position, are in for it. The Republican position, he claims, goes against the grain of the culture, which was moving in a liberal direction on abortion before *Roe v. Wade.* Will's political judgment is unequivocal: "If *Roe* is reversed, either the Republican Party must retreat from its nearly categorical opposition to abortion or it will suffer severe reverses in state legislative contests—and hence in its party-building efforts and its hope of someday capturing the House of Representatives."

George Will, lest anyone not know, is a Republican. His partisan interests are understandable and legitimate, but they are not our concern here. In fact, in the relatively short period since *Webster*, action on abortion in the state legislatures presents a very mixed picture. Both prochoice and prolife forces claim the political tide is running in their favor, and it is a mixed picture when one adds up legislative wins and defeats to date. Prior to the Congressional elections of 1990, there was much talk about an electoral "backlash" against the prolife position. Being prochoice, it was said, would be the "silver bullet" of electoral success. After the elections, no more was heard of such talk and the prochoice leadership generally took the line that abortion had not been much of a factor. The major media, overwhelmingly prochoice in their bias, declared the election a toss-up on the abortion question. Not suprisingly, prolife organizations took this as an admission that they had done very well indeed. When in great public debates the opposition declares a contest to be a draw, there is some reason to believe that they know they have suffered a setback.

Beyond the contingencies of this election or that, however, prolife confidence is more plausible if we keep in mind the very structure of the debate itself. Any limitation whatever on the absolute abortion liberty declared by *Roe* is a defeat for the prochoice position. That is the point driven home by Laurence Tribe of Harvard law school in his 1990 legal and political manual for the prochoice movement, *Abortion: The Clash of Absolutes*. Tribe astutely contends that the debate must be kept focused on the woman rather than the fetus, on who makes the choice rather than the nature of the choice made. Once the public debate is permitted to shift from "a woman's right to choose," Tribe says in effect, the jig is up. The public debate is shifting.

The argument about what comes after *Roe*, however, goes far beyond what happened last year or will happen next. The argument engages questions at four levels, each entangled with the others: the moral, the legal, the cultural, and the political. No doubt the question of the "legal status" of unborn life will depend upon a democratic judgment about, as Will puts it, the "moral significance" of that life. Will thinks some differences can be split "if the argument is not about when in pregnancy life begins but when in pregnancy abortions should stop." That may sound attractive, until it is seen that it redirects the argument to one of the rocks on which *Roe* was dashed. Will himself admits that *Roe*'s differentiations into trimesters—based upon notions such as "viability," and the distinction between "potential" and "meaningful" life—were logically incoherent and contrary to biological, never mind moral, fact.

His proposed recasting of the question is no recasting at all. It simply replays the widely recognized illogic of *Roe*. With respect to the unborn, the question is, What is this? Maybe the question is, Who is this? Most people recognize that the "what" is human life which, barring natural misfortune or deliberate attack, will become the "who" of a person possessing rights. Certainly the question is not "when." Time lines that allow innocent life to be attacked at one point but not at another cannot help but appear to be arbitrary, because in fact they are arbitrary.

The abortion argument has been put through the chronological grinder for years, indeed for centuries. The effort to determine the point of "ensoulment," or of "quickening," or of when a human life becomes a "person" has been exhausted. It is long past time to give it up altogether. In addition to the theological and ethical experience with such debates, contemporary science powerfully underscores the impossibility of making a rational determination of a "before" and "after" with respect to the "moral significance" and hence the "legal status" of unborn life. Of course there are purely emotive and subjective time differentiations that can be made.

Clifford Grobstein, a noted biologist and prochoice advocate, writes in *Science and the Unborn*[2] that we may be able to designate the point at which we can "mobilize interest and concern" for the unborn. At, say, three weeks the life in the womb does not *seem* to many people to be a baby, whereas at, say, twenty weeks they have no doubt about the presence of an unborn child. But this is entirely subjective. It says nothing about what or who is there; it is only a comment on what or who many people *feel* is there. Such feelings are not politically inconsequential, but Grobstein's approach is finally an exercise in raw emotivism. To accept it would gravely jeopardize the moral credibility of laws regarding persons and rights in connections other than abortion. We wisely resist the notion that human rights and constitutional rights are based on the shifting sand of how we *feel* about those who claim such rights, or for whom such rights are claimed.

The abortion debate is not over chronology but over the weighing of a human life against the reasons for terminating that life. The radical prochoice position (i.e., the position of *Roe*) is that *any* consideration is sufficient to justify the decision to terminate. Indeed no reason need be given: the mere wish to terminate is reason enough to terminate. A more moderate prochoice position is that at least *some* reason must be given, and the reason should not be trivial or willful. As the abortion debate comes to a boil in state legislatures, the debate will be over what reasons, if any, justify the decision to terminate.

Are we then in a position, as George Will puts it, of "splitting differences"? Yes and no. Post-*Roe* accommodations will be made in most states. The accommodation already agreed to by most prolife leadership is not on the "moral significance" of the unborn but on the limits of law. The distinction between the legal and the moral is firmly rooted in almost all traditions of ethical reflection, religious or otherwise. It is a distinction, not a separation. Laws must be legitimated by reference to morality, but if we try to translate all of morality into law, we overburden the law, with the result that the law is brought into disrepute. The consistent prolife position is that every unborn human life should be protected by law, without exception. The consensus in the prolife leadership, however, is that there will be exceptions. The reluctant acceptance of that reality in no way implies approval of it. Nor does it indicate inconsistency with respect to the "moral significance" of unborn life. Rather, such acceptance is based on a prudential judgment that combines considerations that are moral, legal, cultural, and political.

After *Roe*, it seems likely that most states will make exceptions for rape, incest, and direct threat to the life of the mother. The political fact is that most prolife leaders, in the movement and in public office, have decided that this is the most that is obtainable in most states. There is also a matter of principle supporting the exception of direct threat to the life of the mother. No law can properly require heroic virtue. For a woman to surrender her life for the life of her unborn child is heroic virtue. One may argue that such self-surrendering love is morally mandated, but it cannot be legally mandated. Saints are produced by divine inspiration, not by edict of the state. Plus, there is a substantial part of the Judeo-Christian tradition that justifies the taking of human life in such extreme, and extremely rare, circumstances.

Rape and incest do not constitute the same life-*versus*-life dilemma. Yet most prolife thinkers have accepted the inevitability of these exceptions as well. To require a woman or girl to carry to term the child of a rapist or a drunken father would be politically unsustainable. Pro-abortionists would certainly exploit such cases in order to undermine the entire proposition that the state has a responsibility to protect the unborn. In addition, the argument can be made that the question of heroic virtue and the limits of law is engaged also in instances of pregnancy from rape or incest. The circumstance of the pregnancy does not affect the nature of the who or what that is the pregnancy. However, diminished responsibility or no responsibility for being pregnant has a bearing on responsibility for the pregnancy. Again, we are dealing with extreme cases. Legislators worry about a rape exception being subject to widespread abuse, since anyone can claim that a pregnancy resulted from rape. After *Roe*, there will no doubt be many efforts to design safeguards against such abuse. But the reality is that exceptions for rape and incest will be allowed almost everywhere. Those whose concern is to protect the unborn will recognize that the requirements of morality, the limits of law, and the possibilities of politics do not always make for the coherence we may desire.

Prolife activists are frequently nervous about discussing the accommodations that may follow the effective reversal of *Roe*. Given our society's adversarial polity, some believe that not an inch should be given, and certainly not even a fraction of an inch should be given in advance. They contend that, state by state, the prolife cause should go for broke. That viewpoint is understandable. By going for broke, however, they could break the remarkable momentum of the prolife movement since *Roe*. It would not be the first time that insistence upon the best defeated the better and perpetuated the worse. And again, in light of the inherent limits of law, it is doubtful that absolute prohibition of abortion is in fact "the best." What, then, is the best that the prolife movement should work for? One answer would seem to be: *The most comprehensive legal protection of the unborn that is culturally and politically sustainable.*

To be sure, we can only discover what is sustainable by historical testing. What is sustainable changes over time, and from place to place. When the law's unlimited license to abort is withdrawn, when the "moral significance" of the unborn again finds support in law, popular attitudes are bound to be affected significantly. The law has a powerful pedagogical effect. The moral confusion of our society is such that many assume that what is legal is also moral. With the law's asserting society's respect for, and interest in, the unborn, the psychological context of the "abortion alternative" will be changed. Absent a "constitutional right" to abortion, the natural disposition to give the benefit of the doubt to life will, it seems probable, reassert itself.

Such a change in attitudes as the result of change in law will affect not only those seeking abortions but also those doing abortions. For example, studies indicate that, with few exceptions, abortionists say they would quit the business if what they are doing were no longer legal. There is the fear of criminal punishment but, much more importantly, of social opprobrium. Common fatuities to the contrary, laws represent moral judgments. Even when those judgments cannot be effectively enforced, they can be effectively taught, and the law is one of society's most potent teaching instruments.

No thoughtful person believes that after *Roe* there will be no more abortions. In this instance, too, where laws are made laws are broken. That is a truism, and has never been a good argument for not making laws. It is a valid caution against the making of unnecessary laws. After almost twenty years of experiment with the abolition of abortion law, it is clear beyond reasonable doubt that a politically effective majority of the American people believes that some measures are necessary to protect the unborn. If the restoration of abortion law will not eliminate abortions, however, one may ask what it will achieve. The hope is that it will bring about two monumental changes.

First, it will effect a drastic reduction in the absolute number of innocent human lives unjustly taken. It is quite possible that there would still be a hundred thousand or more abortions in America each year. And quite possibly, as some claim, there would be many fewer. Nobody can know. What we do know is that, even if we accept a high figure of two hundred thousand, that is 1.4 million fewer than the number of unborn children killed each year under *Roe*. If one believes that each of those unborn children is endowed by "Nature and Nature's God" with a life to live, such a change cannot help seeming a good beyond measure. Every abortion is a tragedy, but more than a million fewer tragedies each year is an extraordinary change for the better.

Hysterical propaganda notwithstanding, this will not mean a return to the clothes-hanger and the back-alley perils of desperate women seeking abortion. Dr. Bernard Nathanson, the pioneer abortionist who became a prolife champion, has explained in detail how the horror stories and statistics invoked to support liberalized abortion in the 1960s were frequently sheer inventions by himself and others.[3] Moreover, the technology since developed by the abortion industry is relatively inexpensive, available, and medically safe (for the mother, not the fetus). Nor, despite the alarums of pro-abortionists, are we facing the post-*Roe* prospect of women being jailed for seeking or obtaining abortions. The prochoice activists would have us believe that abortion law is something alien to our experience, something resuscitated from the "dark ages" of medieval oppression. In fact, the novel thing, the thing that no Western society had attempted before *Roe*, is the total abolition of abortion law. On the basis of long experience prior to *Roe*, it should be obvious that restored abortion law will carry criminal penalties aimed only at the abortionist.

The second great change will be a return to an inclusive definition of membership in the community for which we accept public responsibility. Such a change is urgently needed, and for reasons that go beyond abortion. Witness current agitations for euthanasia and the elimination of categories of people who are, in the lethal logic of *Roe*, not living "meaningful human lives." The elimination of the useless aged, the hopelessly handicapped, and the persistently vegetative is not a matter of alarmist scenarios for the future. Such eliminations are being proposed and, to some extent, are being perpetrated now.

As discussed in earlier chapters, these developments have everything to do with the ominous turn that liberalism took early in the abortion debate. American-style liberalism is schizophrenic. On the one side, it is profoundly communitarian; on the other, radically individualistic. In the abortion debate, the prochoice forces successfully seized the liberal banner for a radical individualism that, in the pursuit of self-actualization, acknowledges no bonds of community or duty to others. In this view, duty is a synonym for oppression. That is the individualism enshrined in *Roe*'s dubious invocation of a constitutional "right to privacy." When communal bonds are thus sundered, public protection is withdrawn not only from the unborn. Proponents of euthanasia, of fetal farming and experimentation, and of the eugenic elimination of the unfit are entirely correct in appealing to the letter and spirit of *Roe*. The reversal of that decision, then, will dramatically reduce the incidence of abortion, and will at least slow the extension of practices that are fully warranted by its reasoning.

So what are we to say to Mr. Will's argument that prochoice and prolife advocates "can split some differences if the argument is not about when in pregnancy life begins but when in pregnancy abortions should stop"? The prolife movement has already made accommodations, but they are not accommodations on the "when" or the "what" or the "who" of human life. They are accommodations that recognize the limits of law in relation to morality. As for splitting differences, one notes that the prochoice advocates have indicated not the slightest willingness to accommodate. The National Organization for Women, Planned Parenthood, ACLU, Laurence Tribe, et al. have adopted an unrelenting posture of "not one inch." Perhaps sensing that they are on the losing side, they fear that the smallest hint of willingness to accommodate would precipitate the entire collapse of the victory they once thought secured by *Roe*.

In a democratic polity such as ours, it is generally best when conflicts can be resolved without total winners and total losers. After *Roe*, the prolife position will hardly have a total victory. There will be some abortions by legal exception, there will be a substantial number of illegal abortions, and it is likely that a few states will permit something close to abortion on demand. Such a situation is hardly satisfactory from the prolife viewpoint. The prolife goal will be to continue to work toward the most comprehensive sustainable legal protection for the unborn, and toward a more caring and sexually responsible society that will reduce the felt need for abortion.

If the post-*Roe* situation will not be satisfactory to prolifers, however, it will be much less satisfactory to prochoicers. There is no blinking the fact that in that situation they will be the primary losers. Mr. Will correctly says, "This democratic nation needs a vigorous argument, not judicial fiat, about abortion." The prochoice cause won two decades of victory by judicial fiat. It became evident in time, however, that they had lost the argument by their stubborn refusal even to acknowledge the question of the "moral significance and hence the proper legal status of life in its early stages." With that stubborn refusal, they set themselves against clear reason and scientific fact—and against the moral sensibilities and common sense of most Americans. On the most critical issue, the "vigorous argument" that Mr. Will calls for is taking place, and it seems that the prolife position is prevailing by default. As discussed in the last chapter, there are very good reasons why the prochoice movement has, in the words of Daniel Callahan, "been unwilling to trust the moral issues to public debate."

The analysis of George Will and others must be challenged also in connection with cultural directions and political consequences. Will writes, "The culture was moving [in a pro-abortion direction] before the Court moved." That was true of the elite culture of the knowledge class. On abortion, the elite culture took the more democratic culture by surprise. It was a while before the democratic culture was able to organize its response to the attack, but the years following are the story of that stunningly effective response. That response is the more impressive when we again recall that the prolife cause had arrayed against it every institution of the Establishment in the media, academe, and religion. The only exception was the Roman Catholic Church, which, then and now, is thought to be very questionably part of the Establishment. Later, in the latter part of the 1970s, the Catholic bishops would be joined by the evangelical and fundamentalist forces that are most definitely not of the Establishment. In American history, there is likely no comparable movement of social change—not abolition, not prohibition, not civil rights—that was able to make such an impact without having friends in the high places of what Mr. Will calls "the culture."

Moreover, many in the elite culture who favored "abortion reform" in the 1960s were later repulsed by the reality of 1.6 million abortions per year. That, they began to say, was not what they had in mind at all. The prolife movement has benefited greatly by the recruitment or acquiescence of these "abortion reformers" who came to have second and third thoughts about abortion-as-contraception and the consequent debasement of human life and communal bonds. Significant changes are evident in mainline/

oldline churches such as the Episcopal, United Methodist, and Presbyterian (U.S.A.). Once on the cutting edge of "abortion reform," they are now trying to make it clear that they are opposed to the present situation of abortion on demand. Groups such as Presbyterians for Life and NOEL (National Organization of Episcopalians for Life), once marginal and barely tolerated in their churches, now have the initiative in changing their denominations' position on abortion. This does not mean that these churches are likely to become strongly prolife any time soon, but neither are they the reliable chaplaincies to the prochoice movement that they once were. In addition, those churches that were "right from the start"—e.g., Roman Catholic and Missouri Synod Lutheran—feel vindicated and possess a new confidence about the role they have played and will play.

The elite culture, once solidly pro-abortion, has been fragmented as the actual consequences of *Roe* have become brutally apparent. In the last chapter, we alluded to Robin Toner's insightful observation about the "two Americas," which she describes as the linguistic community of "rights and laws" *versus* the linguistic community of "rights and wrongs." The momentum in the abortion debate would seem to be in a direction favorable to the prolife position. This has to do with more than the reading of polling data. Yet over the last decade and more, there has been a remarkable stability in popular attitudes. A careful examination of the survey research indicates that about 20 percent of respondents favor prohibiting abortion in every circumstance, about 20 percent favor the unqualified abortion liberty of *Roe*, and about 60 percent say that unborn life should be legally protected, with exceptions for hard cases. When it is explored what respondents mean by "hard cases," it turns out that the exceptions would be very limited indeed.

We should not be surprised to discover that, in the heat of the contest, both sides are sometimes less than candid in the use of polling data. "A Majority of Americans Want Abortion to be the Woman's Choice." "A Majority of

Americans Would Protect Unborn Children by Law." Both headlines are true. It depends on what study you read and what questions were asked. There are studies that show that a majority wants abortion to be the woman's decision, and the same majority, in the same survey, says that abortion is murder. The conclusion to be drawn from such studies is that a majority of Americans think murder should be legal, which seems somewhat improbable. There are other studies indicating that a large majority wants abortion to be a free choice, but then, when asked the circumstances in which abortion should be legal, sharply limit that choice.

A careful analysis of the survey research data over the last two decades leads to two conclusions: First, roughly 75 percent of Americans believe that abortion should not be legal for the reasons that 95 percent of abortions are actually obtained; and, second, the aforementioned distribution of 20–20–60 has not changed much over the years. That means that the "battle for the hearts and minds" of the people is mainly with that 60 percent that wants some kind of accommodation. Because they want an accommodation, they do not identify with the monolithic don't-give-an-inch leadership of the prochoice movement, but neither do they want to be identified with what the media conventionally portray as a stridently rigorist prolife movement. Being for the most part nice people, in the peculiarly American way of niceness, most people want babies to be protected, women to have a choice, and everyone to be happy. In sum, they want the abortion debate to go away. But, of course, that will not happen.

No doubt there will be powerful cultural resistance to legal changes protecting the unborn. But the resistance comes overwhelmingly from sectors of the elite culture that are bitterly disappointed that the "judicial fiat" of *Roe* did not hold. In legislative battles in the several states, the result will be an intensification of the class-based *Kulturkampf* in which our public life is now embroiled. To call it a *Kulturkampf* is no exaggeration: it is a war over the moral definition of American culture. It is the kind of contest with which most politicians are profoundly uncomfortable. A politician in high national office privately put it this way: "When I first ran in the early seventies, all of us knew there was a big debate over abortion, and you had to take a side. That wasn't hard. All you had to do was announce that you were prochoice or prolife, and then you could count on the troops of one side or the other to make the public argument for you. Now that abortion is being returned to the political arena, that has changed. All of a sudden *we* have to explain our positions in public, and most of us are pretty uncomfortable with that because we aren't very good at it, and we aren't very good at it because, frankly, we haven't thought about it very carefully."

Nobody can predict with any confidence the political consequences of the continuing debate over abortion. Mr. Will and others say Republicans must retreat from their prolife position or abandon their hopes of controlling state legislatures and thus of capturing the House of Representatives. The fortunes of the Republican Party are not among the worries that give me sleepless nights, but here, too, I expect that these political observers may be in error. In the 1988 presidential election as many as one-third of the voters said that abortion was their number-one concern—and that one-third overwhelmingly voted Republican. (The numbers may be higher, for it is well known that people tend to avoid giving "controversial" answers to pollsters. To say that abortion is your primary concern is to risk being controversial.) No doubt, as political analysts have claimed, some people voted Republican *despite* the prolife position of the party. The evidence, however, is that in recent elections a great many people voted for Republicans *because of* —or at least *also* because of—their promise to work for the protection of the unborn.

A common lament of Republicans is that they cannot do their presidential trick in congressional and state races because Democrats there are shielded from the ideological issues that win nationally, such as abortion. It is more than arguable that returning the abortion question to the states may be precisely what the Republicans need. Again, our concern is not for the fate of the Republican Party. It is troubling, however, that abortion has so hardened the polarization between parties. In the early 1990s, national Republican leaders talked publicly about the need to "enlarge the tent" of the party to make room for those who take a prochoice position. In fact, the Republicans have been far from monolithic on abortion since *Roe*, and there are many prochoice Republican officeholders, also at the national level. The truly monolithic party on this question is the Democratic Party, in which nobody with national ambitions can deviate one iota from the prochoice line. Perhaps such partisan polarization is unavoidable, but it is nonetheless troubling. It is reminiscent of what became the polarization between political parties over slavery in the last century, and that analogy carries intimations of a *Kulturkampf* that could become very nasty indeed.

As the abortion debate is returned to the states, it might be thought that the prochoice proponents are pretty much in the position they were in back in the 1960s, pressing for the most "liberal" abortion laws they can get. But that is not quite the case. Now they will no longer be the vanguard advocating what is new and progressive. They will be the old guard, defending the discredited *status quo ante* under *Roe*. The prolife proponents, on the other hand, cannot now be taken by surprise. They are formidably organized, they have thousands of seasoned activists, and they possess the confidence that comes from having taken on the establishments and, against all odds, having won critical victories—not least of which is reopening the debate that *Roe* was to have definitively closed. More than that, they are convinced that they are on the side of the angels, and most Americans who are open to the existence of angels tend to agree. (One of the most consistently striking findings in the relevant research is the high correlation between religious commitment and support for the prolife position.) In view of all these factors, it would seem that the prolife movement has every reason for confidence. To be sure, its leaders could still snatch defeat from the jaws of victory, but they would have to work at it.

We are told that, after *Roe*, we will need a civil debate about splitting differences, and there is truth in that. But a civil debate about splitting differences can only happen on the basis of an acknowledgment that the chief difference has already been split. The difference has been split between those who do and those who do not recognize "the moral significance and hence the proper legal status of life in its early stages." That difference has been split in favor of the prolife position. The outcome of that split will, we may expect, be further ratified by the Supreme Court and then by most state legislatures. Nobody can know precisely what this will mean for abortion law and other measures aimed at protecting vulnerable human life. On the other hand, nobody should doubt that there will be continuing and passionate conflict over this question.

By "this question" is meant the effort to protect the unborn, and our common stake in the outcome of that effort is ominously high. But "this question," it is necessary to emphasize again, extends far beyond the unborn. We are witnessing the return of eugenics, a return driven by technological breakthroughs, but even more powerfully by cultural breakdowns. Euthanasia for the elderly and radically handicapped, population control measures, novel reproductive techniques, fetal experimentation, and genetic engineering—these are among the developments that are relentlessly driving us to ask the most basic questions about the *humanum*, what it means to be human. It may very well be that our constitutional polity and the thinness of our public moral discourse cannot bear such questions. There are already indications that our public life is suffering from moral overload by being forced to address questions for which our polity was not designed and our democratic practices have not prepared us. But the questions will not go away.

The institutional life of movements is often fleeting. Labels and slogans have their day and then disappear. It may well be that ten years from now there will not be movements identified as "prolife" and "prochoice." But the conflict that is at the core of those movements has been joined. That conflict will continue and intensify. As Reinhold Niebuhr would remind us, it is not a conflict between the children of darkness and the children of light. People of integrity and conscience are to be found on both sides, and among those who earnestly want not to take sides. Who knows? Differences may be split, accommodations reached, disagreements fudged, and we may somehow muddle through. That outcome may not be morally satisfying, but it is the kind of thing democracies are good at, when they work. And muddling through, given the human propensity for worse, is not without a modicum of moral dignity.

I am convinced, however, that even the prospect of muddling through depends upon there being many more people than there are at present who recognize and contend against the evil that has been insinuated into our public life. Evil is not a word in our conventional political vocabularies, and perhaps just as well. As the stakes become higher and the conflict deepens, it is the more imperative to control our public rhetoric. The demonic feeds on fanaticism. Not fanatically, but quietly, calmly, reflectively, and self-critically, believing Christians and Jews remind one another of the nature of the conflict in which we are engaged, also in the public order. The Christian way of describing what we are up against is framed by Paul: "For we are not contending against flesh and blood, but against the principalities, against the powers, against the world rulers of this present darkness, against the spiritual hosts of wickedness in the heavenly places" (Ephesians 6). Some who overhear us speaking this way will call it fanaticism.

We should not be surprised by that, for fanaticism is the only word some people have for faith.

A nineteenth-century German historian wrote that every moment of history is equally present to God. Every moment is also equally present to great evil. But there are moments in which great evil bestirs itself with intentions that are discernible to those who have eyes to see. Ours is such a moment. Evil, as is its wont, employs the language of the good to disguise its purposes. In this case it is the great good of choice that hides the greater wrong of what is chosen. It is a tempting shrewdly contrived for a free society that has forgotten that freedom depends upon devotion to more than freedom. The tempting is always fit to the times. In all times, however, the response is pretty much the same among those who have eyes to see what is happening and ears to hear the call to resistance. Like those other rescuers, they say, "We did not start. It started. We had no choice."

8. Law and the Unenforceable

Civilization depends upon obedience to the unenforceable. A teacher told me that a long time ago, and with each passing year the wisdom of it bears in upon me more strongly. If it is true, and I am convinced that it is true, it is reason for both anxiety and confidence. Most of the things that make for a modest chance of getting through this life with a measure of dignity and grace rest upon unspoken rules. Some of them are not even speakable without making them sound trite and somehow false. We all know people of whom we say that for them life is hard, meaning that just living is hard. Nothing comes naturally to them, whether in personal relations, or work, or taking time off to supervise cloud formations. They are in a state of perpetual anxiety about what they are supposed to do, how they are supposed to *be*, and are ever worried about the penalties for not getting it right. They are the kind of people who study an instruction manual for riding a bicycle.

The unspoken and unenforceable are ever so much more important than the articulated and enforceable rules that we call laws. Dr. Johnson, as usual, got it right: "How small, of all that human hearts endure, / That part which laws or kings can cause or cure." Throughout this essay, we have been thinking about the imperatives and limits of politics. The point is that we never get the imperatives right until we understand the limits. We should approach politics, and that part of politics that we call the law, with a determined lightheartedness. Politics and law are too serious to be taken with utmost seriousness. Laws are, or should be, in conversation with truths that do require being taken with utmost seriousness, but the discussion of law itself is a second- or third-order conversation. Great passions should be reserved for activities worthy of them, like falling in love or contemplating the nature of God. A debilitated intellectual culture that is indifferent to the excitement of pondering how many angels can dance on the head of a pin is prone to losing its soul to the excitations of laws and kings.

It is a slight amendment of Dr. Johnson's maxim to observe that, when we make the mistake of thinking that laws and kings can cure what human hearts must endure, laws and kings will surely end up causing a great deal of additional misery to be endured. When we seek to re-place the unenforceable with the enforceable, both come to grief. Consider marriage. A marriage constituted by a contract of rules rather than by a covenant of trust is a marriage designed to destruct. Within the covenant, but only within the covenant, rules have their place. They can simplify and clarify the duties inherent in the relationship of love. But they cannot constitute that relationship. What most importantly constitutes the relationship remains un-enforceable, implicit, tacit, understood, allusive.

In thinking about law and laws, it is important to keep these distinctions in mind. A utopian impulse, one that takes both religious and secular forms, tempts us to think that law and laws can do more than they are able. The most perfect laws most exactly enforced cannot create the good society or the good life. The things that make for goodness lie, for the most part, outside the realm of law and laws. Laws are necessary expedients. They come to the rescue where love fails. At the same time, it is love that impels us to frame laws that come to the rescue. But the society ordered by law is necessarily, in the jargon of classical social science, a *gesellschaft* rather than a *gemeinschaft*. That is to say, laws deal with impersonal and institutionalized relationships, rather than with primary communities of memory and trust. These communities live by love, whereas society's proper business is justice.

The confusion in modern politics between justice and love derives, to a very large extent, from the baneful influence of Jean-Jacques Rousseau. He laid the conceptual foundation for the modern political monism that wants to get it all together before God gets it all together in the coming of his Kingdom. Rousseau proposed the vaulting vision of a universal brotherhood and sisterhood in which the state would execute "the general will," thus, according to him, making each citizen his own legislator. In the name of liberty, equality, and, above all, fraternity—which is to say in the name of love—the guillotine was kept busy day and night. The greatest crimes against humanity have been perpetrated in the name of the politics of communal cohesion—e.g., Stalin, Hitler, Mao, and all too many petty imitators. It is not only the monsters of history, however, who promote the political monism that results from the confusion and conflation of justice and love.

From time to time, politicians and commentators in our society invoke the image of the nation or the city as a family. It has an idealistic ring to it, but it is, upon closer examination, nonsense—and dangerous nonsense at that. Of all institutions, the family is dependent upon the unenforceable. While they might invoke the rhetoric appropriate to more exalted associations, the business of politicians is the enforceable. The difference is painfully evident when the law becomes embroiled in trying to adjudicate conflicts within families that have failed. The courts strive to determine gradations of "affectional obligation" and "emotional bonding," with a competence like to that of an ungainly elephant attempting a pirouette.

As with the family, so with the community of faith. Through Judaism, Christianity received an understanding of community in covenant with the Absolute Future that transcends the community. Christian ecclesiology (the doctrine of the church) continues to have more in common with a Jewish understanding of peoplehood than is commonly recognized. Christian thinkers rightly speak of the church as a "sacrament" to the world. The church, especially as it is gathered in sacramental solidarity by the presence of its Lord, is taken as a model for how the world is to be rightly ordered. The church is indeed a model, but it is a proleptic and anticipatory model, witnessing to a promise that will one day be realized universally. If that eschatological factor is forgotten, if the church is taken to be a presently enforceable model, then the church itself becomes a source of tyranny. The *shalom* of God is the Endtime ahead of time, known to the believing community by faith. It is the peace of God that is different from and infinitely fuller than the *tranquillitas ordinis* (Augustine) that is the best possible ordering of the earthly *polis*. The world's peace is the peace of justice, not of love.

Yet many Christians are not satisfied with that peace. Justice is not enough, they say. They are right. Nothing is enough short of the Kingdom of God, the Messianic Age. That is why Christians pray the emphatically Jewish prayer taught them by Jesus, "Thy Kingdom come." It is commonly said that the political vision shaped by biblical faith must move beyond justice to love. That sounds right, but I am convinced that it is wrong. It is love that compels us to do justice, and to see that justice is done. Why should we care about the doing of justice? Because we are commanded to love our neighbor, even our enemy. Justice is the form that love takes in the arena of politics and laws. We might care about justice for utilitarian reasons of calculated self-interest. We might care about justice because we fear the just judgment of God. We are, however, called to care about justice because we are called to love the neighbor. The doing of justice in all its forms—commutative, retributive, distributive—does not just happen. We have to work at it, constantly. It is the work of love. And, for communities ordered by the enforceable, it is work enough.

It is also the function of love-as-justice to encourage and reward obedience to the unenforceable. Laws cannot create love in the form of altruism, or of friendship, or of passionate devotion, but it can respect such forms of love. The chief way in which laws respect such loves is to respect the social spaces in which they flourish. That is why we have laws protecting parental rights and the free exercise of religion. Law serves love by securing love's immunity from law. This is among the humble but imperative functions of the law. Law thus understood is of a piece with our constitutional order of liberal democracy. In the world of politics, liberal democracy is a synonym for humility. We rightly speak of the dignity of the law. But that dignity depends, as it were, upon the law not standing on its own dignity. Law, when it is puffed up with pride and seeks to encompass all that human hearts endure and all to which human hearts aspire, brings law into disrepute. Then law becomes lawlessness, and to that point we will be returning.

In turning our attention to law and laws, it is well to know what we have in mind. By law I mean the process that produces and sustains the formal and public rules by which we attempt to order our life together. Law is legislating, adjudicating, administering, and negotiating the allocation of rights and duties, in the hope of preventing harm, resolving conflicts, and creating means of cooperation. So law is already understood in terms quite comprehensive.

Everything that we have been saying about politics applies also, of course, to law and laws. Law is not self-legitimating. The very term "self-legitimating" is a nonsense term. Something can only be legitimate by reference to something else. At the risk of seeming pedantic, one notes that the adjective "legitimate" is from the past participle of *legitimare,* which means to make legitimate, and has as its first meaning to be lawfully begotten. It is without meaning to speak of *morally* legitimate law except by reference to the good from which it is begotten and to which it is accountable. Theories that attempt to explain law exclusively in terms of expediency, chance, and calculation of interests should assiduously avoid trying to distinguish between legitimate and illegitimate law. Of course such theories can address what is *procedurally* legitimate, but they cannot address what is substantively or morally legitimate. They cannot, in short, distinguish between what is legal and what is right.

That legitimating point of reference can be described in terms of the metaphysical, the ontological, or the higher good. For present purposes, I choose the term transcendence, which suggests what this legitimating referent *does*; namely, it transcends. Law is not exhaustively encompassed in the immanent. It is not law unto itself. Law unto itself is no law at all. This is obviously true in the everyday workings of society. A person who is a law unto himself is an outlaw. Law by definition must transcend in the sense of being transpersonal, it partakes of the universal. Universality means more than the validity bestowed by the procedures of a society. If the law of a society does not transcend that society, then that society, including its legal procedures, is an outlaw. That is the inescapable claim implicit in, for example, a United Nations *universal* declaration of human rights. Those who deal with questions of legality without reference to the questions of meta-legality might accurately be described as the technicians of outlaw law. Laws, which are penultimate and deal with the enforceable, draw on larger worlds of the ultimate and unenforceable.

To speak of transcendence is, unavoidably, to speak of religion. (It is not necessarily unavoidable at the highly abstracted theoretical level, but it is unavoidable in socio-historical fact.) And to speak of religion is to raise powerful fears about mystification that would carry thinking about the law back to the putatively dark ages of religion's hegemony over public life. Many hold that the story of

the achievement of jurisprudential clarity and "realism" is
the tortuous tale of the liberation of law from the thralldom of religion, metaphysics, and associated prejudices.
Others respond more moderately. They are prepared to
allow that, pushed far enough, laws must be grounded
in a legitimacy other than their own. But, they add, it is
precisely the genius of our constitutional order that the
law need not, and must not, be pushed so far. In their
wisdom the Founders separated the ultimate questions of
the transcendent from the penultimate, and usually less
than prepenultimate, questions of the immanent. It is the
great virtue of our system, they say, that we need not agree
upon the highest good, nor even upon any good, in order
to deliberate about the allocation of rights and duties. With
respect to such lofty and inevitably divisive matters, the
state is blessedly neutral.

That response contains much that is importantly true
and useful. At the same time, it is typically offered to the
end of keeping the public square naked of religiously informed discourse, an end that I have argued is neither possible nor desirable. As we have seen, our dilemma is that,
just as questions that engage ultimacies are more frequently
erupting in the public arena, we discover that we have
no shared vocabulary for addressing such questions. Such
questions of great moral import are commonly erupting
in the courts, precisely that institution in the public arena
from which the language of moral legitimacy has been most
rigorously excluded.

In this connection, we have considered the question of
abortion. As important as the question of abortion is by
itself, it is not by itself. The abortion controversy is the
flashpoint. A flashpoint indicates the degree of flammability
of combustible materials. In this case, the combustible materials are produced by, among other things, a convergence
of technique, on the one hand, and the neglect of legal concepts by which the power of technique can be checked, on
the other. As it happens in our attics and our basements,

so it happens in the ordering of society that combustible materials accumulate by neglect. We tell ourselves that we will get around to them some day, but meanwhile we are terribly busy and they can be, for the time being, safely ignored. Some recognize that the fire has begun and may already be out of control. Others are determined to ignore it, going on with business as usual. Yet others are like Kierkegaard's audience in the theater, wildly applauding the announcement and repeated announcement that the theater is on fire. Some think the announcement is part of the play. Others see that the fire is real enough but welcome the prospect of being relieved of the burden of a life filled with having to go to the theater.

Perhaps the image of a fire is exaggerated, even inflammatory, but I think not. In the treatment of human life at all stages, the structure of our thinking and practice has been gravely weakened. Medical and other techniques rush through legal doors no longer barred by moral judgment. The defining and protecting of rights can be expanded and contracted almost at will. Rights turn out to have no foundation other than the law, and the law, in turn, has no foundation other than that it is the law, which is to say that the law has no foundation. In abortion and other instances, rights are overriden in the name of another right, the right to privacy. At one time in American public life, it may fairly be observed, our highest appeal was to Providence; now it is to privacy. The course of political discourse in two hundred years of our constitutional history is marked by the decline from Providence to privacy. To explain why some thinkers hail this as progress would require another essay on the meaning of decadence.

The logic of *Roe v. Wade* is in many ways a consistent working out of the legal implications of the naked public square. The effort of the court was to distinguish among beings who are indisputably members of the human species. It was decided to bestow the constitutional accolade of personhood on some, and to withhold it from others. The substantive meaning of "person" remains quite unclear. It seems very much like a sentiment, and a rather arbitrary sentiment at that. Further, it is not very helpful to distinguish between "person" and person in "the full meaning" of the term when the term is given no clear meaning to begin with.

Critics of *Roe* may be forgiven for saying that the court has declared that human rights are coterminous with the ability to claim and exercise such rights. The allocation of rights and immunities is separated from any account of a transcendent good or truth. Justice Blackmun, writing for the majority, observed that questions of the good and the true could not be admitted to the deliberation because theologians, philosophers, and others who worry about such things are not in agreement with one another. It might be argued that, by the same token, *Roe* should have been declared null and void because many jurists disagree with it so intensely. If what we disagree about is not justiciable, courts would go out of business. But, of course, courts stay in business, imposing their own disputed judgments while ruling out of order other judgments, also disputed, that they do not care to entertain.

A person, we may be able to agree, is one who is a member of the political community, possessing rights and immunities and entitled to due process of law. Until fairly recently in American history, such membership and attendant rights were thought to be transcendently grounded. Only in this light could they be declared to be, as they were declared to be, "unalienable." But now, against the doctrine of transcendent personhood, is posited the doctrine of *conditional personhood*. The ramifications of the change are truly impressive. Of course, the exercise of certain rights has always been conditioned by notions of the common good or the social contract. But that the persons so restricted, or so restricting themselves, were persons was not in question. The new thing is not that we discriminate between persons in dealing with rights and duties. Every society must do that. The new thing is that beings whom we might otherwise take to be persons are declared to be, in constitutional fact, non-persons. The new thing is not that they are treated differently within the terms of the social contract; it is that they are quite simply erased from the contract. Obviously, the consequences of this new thing extend far beyond the unborn.

I do not deny but readily admit that the "slippery slope" argument has slipped in here. Many protest the suggestion that there is a necessary progression from abortion to infanticide, to eliminating the inconvenient elderly and radically handicapped. "Necessary" is indeed too strong a word. But—*if* a certain measure is proposed, and *if* there is legal license for doing it, and *if* it is technically doable, and *if* it is in the felt interest of those who are in control of the doing of it, why should we think that it will not be done?

One may answer that in a democratic society political license is also required, and it may override the granting of a legal license. "We, the People" may declare the thing proposed to be unacceptably repugnant. But the people can be, as it is said, "educated." Popular intuitions about what is right and what is good can be discredited, at least when they break out of their containers of privacy and impinge inconveniently upon the public realm. Moreover, those who feel it in their interest to do the repugnant thing are themselves of "the people." Those most immediately involved—meaning those who do the thing or have it done, not those *to whom* it is done—are, we are endlessly told, involved in a most private and anguished circumstance. Others, it is said, have no right to interfere in such a "personal decision." Some of the others who might have qualms are persuaded by that reasoning. Most of the others avert their eyes.

The people whom John Rawls has calculating the terms of the social contract are not interested in the good. They are interested only in securing for themselves the "goods"

of society. One wishes that such people existed only behind Mr. Rawls's mythical "veil of ignorance," but we know
too many of them too well. Such people can easily be
persuaded that their interests and the interests of the technicians are one. Those who have qualms about the good
(about rights and wrongs, not just rights and laws) can
be wondrously flexible when qualms are weighed against
the desirability of the goods. Especially is this the case
when the only ones that might get hurt do not yet, or do
no longer, or never can, meet our conditions for being
persons. Those who discount scenarios of the slippery
slope betray an unseemly confidence that people will prefer what is good over what presents itself as *good for them*.

A pundit who works for what some take to be the
greatest newspaper in the world was recently listening to a
discussion of the latest advances in the mapping and alter-
ation of human genes. There was talk about the return of
eugenics and the ineffectiveness of professional bioethics
(which has become little more than a permissions office
for what scientists want to do) in checking the presently
and potentially monstrous. The demand for "the perfect
baby," someone said, leads to intolerance toward babies
and others who are less than perfect. They will not be
tolerated because their being born is no longer necessary.
One discussant suggested that we no longer have freak
shows at country fairs not because we have become more
compassionate but because, in the world of our designing,
there is no place for freaks. And yes, the slippery slope
was mentioned more than once. Finally, our pundit had
had enough. He had heard these discussions before, he
said. He had even read C. S. Lewis on eugenics and "the
abolition of man," and he was unimpressed. There is probably a gene, he said, that makes some people stay awake
at night worrying about such things. He hoped the gene
would soon be discovered, so that it could be altered in
those afflicted by it. Thus did he dismiss the "myth" of the
slippery slope. Science marches on, and down.

There is another image that is helpful in understanding this moment of American cultural, political, and legal thought. It might be described as nihilism without the abyss. Considered only in terms of the history of ideas, we have arrived at the abyss. That is to say, the prevailing patterns of political and legal theory offer no public account of the good. Therefore we cannot publicly speak of "evil" without embarrassment. And again, we have most particularly ruled out of order public accounts of the good that may be grounded in religion. Thus, at least in theory, we arrive at the abyss in which all things are permitted.

Nietzsche was right. George Parkin Grant writes in *English-Speaking Justice*: "Nietzsche's writings may be singled out as a Rubicon, because more than a hundred years ago he laid down with incomparable lucidity that which is now publicly open: what is given about the whole in technological science cannot be thought together with what is given us concerning justice and truth, reverence and beauty, from our tradition. . . . Nietzsche's greatest ridicule is reserved for those who want to maintain a content to 'justice' and 'truth' and 'goodness' out of the corpse that they helped to make a corpse."[1] This is our situation, I believe, if considered only in terms of how ideas operate in our elite culture. Fortunately, the cultural conquest of the knowledge class is by no means complete. Fortunately, there are still institutions, laws, traditions, and what Tocqueville called "habits of the heart" that succeed, some of the time, in holding us back from the abyss in actual life. But all of these are perilously weak if they cannot be defended by public argument that lays claim to being the *truth* of the matter.

By the early part of this century, with the triumph of scientific naturalism, the Lockean-Puritan synthesis had largely lost its hold on intellectual, cultural, and legal elites. The dogma became established that the scientifically guided ordering of society could in no way be held accountable to a necessarily "unscientific" account of the good. There were those who tried to counter that dogma. We have already discussed John Dewey and his "common faith." Robert Hutchins and Mortimer Adler tried to revive a classical tradition of political and legal thought that proposed an account, even a transcendent account, of the good. Leo Strauss, according to some of his disciples, thought the wisdom of Jerusalem should interact with the wisdom of Athens. According to more of his disciples, however, Athens is Athens and Jerusalem is Jerusalem, and never the twain can meet—at least not in public, rational discourse. In the Christian tradition, there were figures such as the Niebuhr brothers, Reinhold and H. Richard. The challenge of World War II and the realities of totalitarianism had a powerfully sobering effect that brought momentary respite from the reign of optimistic scientism over the public mind. It was only momentary.

Soon the nihilists were again in the saddle. To be sure, there were thinkers who recognized that the totalitarian threat had not died with Hitler, but they were generally dismissed as benighted cold warriors. By the 1950s the orthodoxy had been widely reestablished that the "genius" of American politics, including jurisprudence, is that it is "nonideological." Nonideological was taken to mean that there are no systematic or coordinated ideas, certainly no account of the good, by which life together in society is to be ordered. In this sense, the intellectual climate was and is profoundly anti-intellectual. The powers of reason were astutely employed in debunking the authority of reason. The world was not ruled by reason, nor could it be. At best, reason leads us to understand that reality is controlled by mechanical necessity, chance, and irrational impulse. This was the lesson propounded also by numerous "realists" in the theory of law and rights. The "hermeneutics of suspicion" trained us to see that there are the "good" reasons that we give for what we do, and then there are the "real" reasons. The good reasons are self-deceptive, enabling some of us to believe that we are moral actors in what clever people know is an amoral universe. According to this view, no good reason is so thoroughly self-deceptive as the reason that attempts to give an account of the good.

People persist in trying, however, and sometimes the regnant ideas are shaken. The civil rights movement was such a shaking. I mean especially the period from 1956 to 1965, when the movement was under the magisterial direction of Martin Luther King, Jr. That period remains the moral baseline for our thinking about civil rights, and much else, today. Dr. King made the case for civil rights, and for human rights, in a way that was democratically legitimated. He made the case from an account of the good that was manifestly derived from a religious claim of transcendent truth. He contended for the enforcement of the enforceable, invoking the truths of the unenforceable. Popular thought about civil rights today is still living off the moral capital accumulated by the work of Dr. King. Among many of our intellectual grandees, however, the meaning of King and his movement is stripped of the account of the good and the belief system that produced that account. His appeal to transcendent truth, if not ignored entirely, is condescendingly treated as the rhetorical embellishment necessary for mobilizing the incorrigibly religious masses (especially those black folk whose peculiar history of suffering excuses their being so religious). Dr. King generally escaped the criticism that his "good" reasons disguised his "real" reasons because he was, after all, working for a "good cause."

Nonetheless, with respect to regnant nihilisms, the witness of Dr. King shook their foundations—or, more aptly, exposed their lack of foundations. Although the issues are often different, a similar effect is being worked today by the renewed public assertiveness of committed Christians, Jews, and people who simply believe in the possibility of moral reason. This assertiveness should be allowed to do its necessary work of forcing all of us to abandon self-deceptions about value-neutrality and nonideological devotion to easy positivisms. This aggressively moral force in public life can easily degenerate into a movement of vulgar, and even abusive, moralism. That it will do so at times is almost inevitable. But those who are put off by its tone and offended by its policy proposals are then challenged to offer a more winsome and convincing account of the good that makes their own proposals morally compelling.

At the same time, publicly assertive religious forces must be mindful that the remedy for the naked public square is not naked religion in public. Put differently, the alternative to the naked public square is not the religious public square but the civil public square. In Poland, Czechoslovakia, and elsewhere in Eastern Europe after the collapse of communist regimes, the need to rediscover and reconstitute "civil society" became a common refrain. Americans, too, need to relearn the importance of civil society. Civil society depends upon those associations that are not controlled by the government but that make democratic governance possible. Civil society has everything to do with the mediating institutions discussed earlier. These are the communities of memory and mutual aid, of character and moral discipline, of transcendent truth and higher loyalty. Such institutions are by no means all identifiably "religious" in nature, and yet they participate in that deeper communal bonding suggested by the Latin root *religare*.

If they are enduring and deep, these communities develop their own languages, or at least their own dialects. A democratic and pluralistic society does not try to develop a uniform language, a kind of esperanto. Our kind of society requires that citizens be multilingual, not monolingual. American society is best conceived as a community of communities. Citizens move in and out of communities, crossing lines and languages in often confusing ways— confusing to themselves and to others. The resulting dissonance is called democracy. The national community, to the extent it can be called a community, is a very "thin" community. The myriad communities that constitute civil society are where we find the "thick" communities that bear heavier burdens of loyalty.

It may be objected that it is only the national community that is able to elicit the final loyalty of laying down one's life in its defense. That is somewhat misleading. Americans in war have typically fought for "Mom and apple pie," for the defense of the communities within the community, the communities from which the national community derives its worth and for which it exists. In FDR's language, they fought for the "four freedoms" (of speech, of worship, of economic activity, and the freedom from the fear of government tyranny). The idea that people would die for the State or for the Fatherland or Motherland is thoroughly alien to the American spirit. The nation is a thin community whose chief function is to protect the thick communities of deeper allegiance.

Americans who live, then, in diverse communities with diverse languages and diverse ways of dreaming their dreams engage one another in the civil public square. The public philosophy that is needed is precisely a philosophy that sustains that diversity. Such a philosophy is not "a common faith" but a way in which people of diverse faiths can build on what they have in common. The goal is not a moral esperanto. The proponents of liberal universalism deride other moral languages as "sectarian." But there is nothing more sectarian than esperanto. Nobody speaks universal language. People speak languages. In a pluralistic society, we need to be multilingual if we care about the public order. If we know who we are, however, we will know one language to be more our own than any other. The primary language of the Christian, for instance, will be that of scripture, creed, and gospel teaching. It is spoken most fluently and richly in the communities where Christians gather. It can be spoken freely also in the public square, where it engages and challenges, and is engaged and challenged by, other languages.

Many of us are reluctant to abandon the idea of a public esperanto because we fear the consequences. If public discourse is a matter of language vs. language, faith vs. faith, account of the good vs. account of the good, public discourse will fall prey to the curse of Babel. As religious and secular sects combat other religious and secular sects, political debate will become civil war carried on by other means (MacIntyre), and maybe civil war itself. What some call robust democratic pluralism others see as a formula for anarchy. It cannot be denied that the honest public engagement of our diverse particularities is problematic. The result will not be that we all agree with one another. Indeed, there may be more disagreement. But at least we would know what we are disagreeing about, namely, different accounts of the good by which we might order our life together. Recall the words of John Courtney Murray: "The goal is to achieve disagreement. It is a difficult and rare achievement. Most of what we call disagreement is simply confusion."

Against those who would impose their own values in the guise of value-neutrality, democracy is not served by evading the question of the good. A political community is worthy of moral actors only as it engages the question of the good. Against those who fear civil war as a result of particularities in conflict, the account of human nature offered in the language of some communities assures that, since we are all human, we will have a great deal in common. (Admittedly, those whose belief system cannot accommodate the idea of "human nature" have reason to fear the kind of unhindered communication proposed here. They should perhaps reexamine their belief system.) Human commonalities, as well as the shared experience of living together in this kind of society, will assure that there will be, at least for public purposes, considerable "overlap" between different languages and moral traditions. Spheres of "overlap" should be welcomed and cultivated while, at the same time, the scope of "public purposes" should be limited because the "overlap" will always be limited. Rich communal languages are chiefly about the unenforceable, and it is the duty of public law to protect them from the rule of public law.

Against the threat of Babel, anarchy, and civil war, there is also the not inconsiderable factor of a constitutional order by which we have all agreed to abide. (The ways in which later generations "agreed to" the Constitution, and whether those who oppose the constitutional order are protected by that order are subjects of long standing debates that need not delay us here. The happy fact is that almost all Americans understand themselves to have put their signature, as it were, to the Constitution.) Finally, there is the commonality of human reason—the ability to perceive, comprehend, argue, infer, deduce, persuade. To be sure, the nature of reason is a huge subject on which there would seem to be little agreement. In fact, however, there is a clear distinction between those who do and those who do not think there are good reasons to believe in reason. For those who do not believe in reason—the post-Nietzschian nihilists and cultural deconstructionists—public discourse, including dispute over laws and the law, can only be understood in terms of "the will to power."

One hopes, of course, that such people can be persuaded to reexamine their belief system. Absent that, however, their will to power must be checked by the vibrant and unhindered exercise of democratic pluralism. The threat of anarchy and civil war in such vibrant interaction is reduced, I have argued, by commonalities of human nature, of overlapping languages, of shared experience, of tested institutions, of constitutional order, and of capacity for reason. By all these factors the threat is reduced, but not eliminated. At the end of the day, however, what are the alternatives to a vibrantly pluralistic public rendering of accounts of the good? It would seem that there are only two. The first is the domination of a putatively universal account of the good, to be imposed by the allegedly enlightened and disinterested few. That, I have suggested, is the sectarianism of esperanto, an intellectual sleight of hand that has for too long skewed our political and legal discourse. The second possibility is nihilism, which is simply to deny that an account of the good is possible, even if it does seem to be necessary. Those who claim to be speaking esperanto would seem to be on the intellectual defensive today. The nihilists—ironically enough for nihilists—seem to be brimming with confidence that their time has come around at last.

Civilization depends upon obedience to the unenforceable. Public law deals with the enforceable. Because the unenforceable—virtue, honor, discernment, decency, compassion, and hope—is ever so much more important, the sphere of law must be limited as much as possible. For reasons we have discussed in these chapters, that sphere is today expanding. In such a situation, love in the form of justice must attend to those who are most vulnerable to the law when the law is not accountable to the good. Justice requires that we hold the law accountable, and that task requires the engagement of those who have been formed by communities that know a justice better than the justice of which the earthly *polis* is capable.

One cannot help but be keenly aware that some think it is too late to attempt a publicly potent account of the good. There are compelling reasons to resist that conclusion. Ours is a moment of nihilism without the abyss, or at least of only partial descent into the abyss. Perhaps the further descent is inevitable, perhaps there is no place to get even a temporary footing that might make a public difference. History is filled with the rise and fall of civilizations, and we have no reason to think that we are immune to the turnings of time. In that case, we may hope that the abyss is not infinite and we might one day find our way to the other side. But still on this side of the last descent, there are laws, institutions, traditions, habits of the heart, and capacities of the mind that can hold us back. It may be possible to stop the descent and even to gain higher ground. Whether that is possible depends, no doubt, on many factors. It depends on no factor so critically as the free and unhindered engagement in public of alternative accounts of a transcendent good by which we should order our life together. Civil discussion of the enforceable might yet be renewed by respect for the unenforceable, upon which the continued existence of the *civitas* depends.

Then again, it really may be too late. There is no sure answer to that, except to say with Eliot, "For us, there is only the trying. The rest is not our business."

Notes

INTRODUCTION

1. Jaroslav Pelikan, *The Vindication of Tradition* (Yale University Press, 1984).

CHAPTER ONE

1. New class theory, or knowledge class theory, has been around for some time but has not yet received as thorough an elaboration as it warrants. Irving Kristol first introduced the term to political discourse in *Two Cheers for Capitalism* (Basic Books, 1978). Variations on the theory are examined in Barry Bruce-Briggs, editor, *The New Class?* (Transaction, 1979), and the pertinent ideas are explored from a distinctly leftist perspective in Alvin Gouldner, *The Future of Intellectuals and the Rise of the New Class* (Seabury Press, 1979). Perhaps the most succinct and useful treatment of the knowledge class phenomenon is in chapter three ("Class: The Ladder of Success") of Peter Berger's *The Capitalist Revolution* (Basic Books, 1986). The role of the knowledge class in the *Kulturkampf* under consideration here is also discussed in James Davison Hunter's *Culture Wars: The Struggle to Define America* (Basic Books, 1991). Although in his study he is painstakingly careful not to "take sides" in the culture wars, Hunter's sociological analysis is very close to the reading of contemporary American life that underlies my argument in this book.

2. On politics as a Christian vocation, see Richard John Neuhaus, *Christian Faith and Public Policy* (Augsburg, 1977). For the continuing pertinence of Reinhold Niebuhr's understanding of power and moral ambiguity, see Richard John Neuhaus, editor, *Reinhold Niebuhr Today* (Eerdmans, 1989).

3. Robert Wuthnow, *The Restructuring of American Religion*, (Princeton University Press, 1988).

4. H. Richard Niebuhr, *The Social Sources of Denominationalism* (Henry Holt & Co., 1929).

5. Vernard Eller, *Christian Anarchy: Jesus' Primacy Over the Powers* (Eerdmans, 1987).

6. On Jewish and Christian understandings of covenant see Leon Klenicki and Richard John Neuhaus, *Believing Today: Jew and Christian in Conversation* (Eerdmans, 1989).

CHAPTER TWO

1. Ernst Cassirer, *The Myth of the State* (Yale University Press, 1946).

2. For Leo Strauss's view of Burke see *Edmund Burke and the Natural Law* (University of Michigan, 1958). Also, Alexander Bickel, *The Morality of Consent* (Yale University Press, 1975).

3. John Hallowell, *The Moral Foundation of Democracy* (University of Chicago Press, 1954).

4. John Dewey, *A Common Faith* (Yale University Press, 1934).

5. Richard Rorty, *Contingency, Irony, and Solidarity* (Cambridge University Press, 1989). For a more complete discussion of Rorty's argument see Richard John Neuhaus, "Joshing Richard Rorty," *First Things* (December 1990).

6. On the perduring role of religion in American public life and religion as an "independent variable," see Richard John Neuhaus, editor, *Unsecular America* (Eerdmans, 1986). That volume contains an analytical summary of relevant survey research data in support of the argument offered here.

7. For a fuller analysis of Protestant "reconstructionism" that proposes a "biblical blueprint" for reconstituting society, see Richard John Neuhaus, "Why Wait for the Kingdom? The Theonomist Temptation," *First Things* (May 1990.)

8. David Novak treats the Noahide commandments and their relation to public morality in *The Image of the Non-Jew in Judaism* (Edwin Mellon Press, 1983) and in *Jewish-Christian Dialogue* (Oxford University Press, 1989).

9. Max Stackhouse has set forth his argument for a "public theology" in several forms, perhaps most succinctly in "An Ecumenist Plea for a Public Theology," *This World*, no. 8 (Spring-Summer 1984).

10. Henry F. May examines varieties of Enlightenment thought that contributed to the American experiment in *The Enlightenment in America* (Oxford University Press, 1976).

11. Walter Lippmann's *Essays in the Public Philosophy*, published in 1955, is recently reprinted as *The Public Philosophy* (Transaction Books, 1989).

12. On the common tradition of philosophy, see Alasdair MacIntyre, "Philosophy, the 'Other' Disciplines and Their Histories: A Rejoinder to Richard Rorty," in *Soundings* 65, no. 2 (Summer 1982).

CHAPTER THREE

1. On Dr. King's theological training, see Taylor Branch, *Parting the Waters* (Simon and Schuster, 1988); especially chapter three, "Niebuhr and the Pool Tables."

2. Norman Podhoretz, *Breaking Ranks* (Harper & Row, 1979).

3. Richard John Neuhaus, "The Loneliness of the Long-Distance Radical," *Christian Century* (April 26, 1972).

4. Peter L. Berger and Richard J. Neuhaus, *Movement and Revolution* (Doubleday, 1970).

5. Mitchell Goodman, *The Movement Toward a New America* (Knopf, 1970).

6. Daniel Berrigan and Robert Coles, *The Geography of Faith* (Beacon Press, 1972).

CHAPTER FOUR

1. Daniel P. Moynihan, *Maximum Feasible Misunderstanding* (Free Press, 1969).

2. The mediating structures paradigm was set forth by Peter Berger and myself in *To Empower People: The Role of Mediating Structures in Public Policy* (American Enterprise Institute, 1977). I take up the mediating structures question with

specific reference to Catholic social teaching and the ideas of Pope John Paul II in a forthcoming book, tentatively titled *Doing Well & Doing Good: The Moral Challenge of the Free Economy* (Doubleday).

3. William Julius Wilson, *The Truly Disadvantaged* (University of Chicago Press, 1987).

4. Charles Murray, *Losing Ground* (Basic Books, 1984) and *In Pursuit of Happiness and Good Government* (Simon and Schuster, 1988).

5. Edward C. Banfield, *The Unheavenly City* (Little, Brown, 1968).

CHAPTER FIVE

1. Samuel P. Oliner and Pearl M. Oliner, *The Altruistic Personality* (Free Press, 1988).

2. Philip Hallie, *Lest Innocent Blood Be Shed* (Harper & Row, 1978).

3. I have set out the framework for the argument regarding the necessary connection between religion and public philosophy in *The Naked Public Square: Religion and Democracy in America* (Eerdmans, 1984).

4. Klaus Scholder, *The Churches and the Third Reich*, vol. 1 (Fortress, 1988). This is, I believe, the best treatment of how the churches responded to Nazism, especially in the years leading up to World War II. Regrettably, Scholder died at an early age and was unable to continue the story through to the end of the Third Reich.

CHAPTER SIX

1. Mary Ann Glendon, *Abortion and Divorce in Western Law* (Harvard University Press, 1987).

2. Laurence Tribe, *Abortion: The Clash of Absolutes* (Norton, 1990).

3. Richard John Neuhaus, "Abortion: The Dangerous Assumptions," *Commonweal* (June 21, 1967).

4. Paul R. Ehrlich, *The Population Bomb* (Ballantine, 1968).

5. Kristen Luker, *Abortion and the Politics of Motherhood* (University of California Press, 1984). The best single analysis of survey research and related sociological data is James Davison Hunter's "What Americans Really Believe About Abortion," *First Things* (June 1992).

6. Faye D. Ginsburg, *Contested Lives* (University of California Press, 1989).

7. Daniel Callahan, *Abortion: Law, Choice, and Morality* (Macmillan, 1970).

8. Daniel Callahan, "An Ethical Challenge to Prochoice Advocates," *Commonweal* (November 23, 1990).

9. The *New York Times* and *Wall Street Journal* editorials appeared, respectively, on December 27 and December 28, 1990.

CHAPTER SEVEN

1. George Will, "Splitting Differences," column in *Newsweek* (February 13, 1989).

2. Clifford Grobstein, *Science and the Unborn* (Basic Books, 1988).

3. Bernard Nathanson, *Aborting America* (Doubleday, 1979). Nathanson, who established one of the largest abortion clinics in the country before his conversion to the prolife cause, provides a singular insider's account of how the pro-abortion movement was launched with such remarkable success.

CHAPTER EIGHT

1. George Parkin Grant, *English-Speaking Justice* (University of Notre Dame Press, 1985).

Index

197